ADOBE PREMIERE PRO 2024 USER GUIDE

A Step-by-Step Handbook to Effectively Learn the Basic Features and Tools in Premiere Pro 2024

DANIEL M. LARRY

Copyright 2024 @ Daniel M. Larry

TABLE OF CONTENTS

DISCLAIMER

The contents of this book are provided for informational and entertainment purposes only. The author and publisher make no representations or warranties with respect to the accuracy, applicability, completeness, or suitability of the contents of this book for any purpose.

The information contained within this book is based on the author's personal experiences, research, and opinions, and it is not intended to substitute for professional advice. Readers are encouraged to consult appropriate professionals in the field regarding their individual situations and circumstances.

The author and publisher shall not be liable for any loss, injury, or damage allegedly arising from any information or suggestions contained within this book. Any reliance you place on such information is strictly at your own risk.

Furthermore, the inclusion of any third-party resources, websites, or references does not imply endorsement or responsibility for the content or services provided by these entities.

Readers are encouraged to use their own discretion and judgment in applying any information or recommendations contained within this book to their own lives and situations.

Thank you for reading and understanding this disclaimer.

CHAPTER ONE
Introduction

Overview of Adobe Premiere Pro

Video editing involves working with source files, including video and graphics obtained from the internet or captured with a camera, and then manipulating, combining, and organizing them to create a final project. This could be anything from a film to a commercial to an instructional video or any other type of video content. Adobe Premiere Pro is a comprehensive software solution available for both Windows and Mac, offering a suite of tools necessary for editing high-quality videos professionally.

Adobe Premiere Pro is a professional-grade video editing software application. It's widely considered the industry standard for editing videos for film, TV, web, and social media.

Here's a quick rundown of Premiere Pro:

- **Timeline-based editing:** Premiere Pro uses a timeline interface where you arrange and edit your video clips.
- **Powerful features:** It has a vast range of tools for editing, colour correction, adding effects, and audio mixing.
- **Part of Creative Cloud:** Premiere Pro is part of the Adobe Creative Cloud suite, which means it integrates well with other Adobe programs like Photoshop and After Effects.

- **Subscription model:** You can't buy Premiere Pro outright; it's available through a monthly or annual subscription to Creative Cloud. There's a free trial available if you want to test it out before you commit.

When assessing Adobe Premiere Pro, it's essential to weigh both its strengths and weaknesses to provide a comprehensive review.

Here's a breakdown of the pros and cons of using Adobe Premiere Pro:

Pros of Adobe Premiere Pro:

- **Abundance of AI-powered tools:** Adobe Premiere Pro offers a wide array of AI-powered features that streamline the video editing process, making tasks more efficient and less time-consuming.
- **Automatic transcription:** The software provides automatic transcription capabilities, allowing users to generate text transcripts of their audio tracks, which can be helpful for accessibility and editing purposes.
- **Copy and paste effects:** Premiere Pro enables users to easily copy and paste effects within the timeline, facilitating quick adjustments and edits across multiple clips.
- **Learning mode:** The platform includes a learning mode feature designed to help new users navigate the software and learn its functionalities effectively, easing the learning curve.
- **Auto-reframe:** Adobe Premiere Pro offers an auto-reframe feature that automatically adjusts videos to different aspect ratios, optimizing them for various platforms and devices.

Cons of Adobe Premiere Pro:

- **Limited audio library:** One drawback of Adobe Premiere Pro is the absence of an extensive free audio or sound effects library, requiring users to source their audio assets elsewhere.
- **Restrictions with generative fill:** The generative fill feature in Premiere Pro has limitations, as it doesn't allow for the creation of movable objects and lacks advanced lighting controls.
- **Intimidating interface:** For beginners, the interface of Adobe Premiere Pro can be intimidating and overwhelming due to its extensive features and complexity.

- **Dependency on additional programs/plugins:** Some advanced techniques, such as effects and generative fill, may require users to purchase additional programs or plugins, adding to the overall cost and complexity of the editing process.

In summary, while Adobe Premiere Pro offers numerous benefits for professional video editing, including AI-powered tools and efficient workflows, it also has drawbacks such as a limited audio library and a steep learning curve for beginners. Understanding these pros and cons can help users make informed decisions when considering Adobe Premiere Pro as their primary video editing platform.

Who Uses Premiere Pro?

Premiere Pro is utilized by a diverse range of professionals, including filmmakers, television broadcasters, marketing agencies, students, and anyone else requiring video editing capabilities.

It's widely regarded as one of the top professional video editing software packages on the market today. Despite the popularity of other tools like Apple Final Cut Pro and Avid's Media Composer, Premiere Pro stands out as the industry standard for video editing. Premiere Pro caters to a wide range of video editing needs, so it's used by many professionals.

Here are some of the main users:

- **Video Editing Firms:** These companies specialize in creating video content for clients, and Premiere Pro is their go-to tool for editing commercials, documentaries, and other projects.
- **Broadcast Media:** News stations and TV production companies use Premiere Pro for editing news footage, shows, and commercials.
- **Marketing and Advertising Professionals:** Creating engaging video content is crucial for marketing these days, and Premiere Pro helps design teams and marketing specialists edit social media videos, product demos, and explainer videos.
- **Filmmakers:** While not exclusive to Hollywood, Premiere Pro is used for editing feature films, independent movies, and even big-budget productions.
- **Educators and Students:** Many schools teach video editing with Premiere Pro due to its industry standard status, and educators use it to create video lectures or presentations.

Even hobbyists and YouTubers can leverage Premiere Pro to edit their videos with professional-looking results.

Importance of Video Editing Software

Video editing software is vital for transforming raw footage into polished and impactful videos. *Here's why it's important:*

- **Crafting a Cohesive Narrative:** Imagine a movie without editing - it would be a jumble of scenes. Editing software lets you arrange clips, cut out unnecessary portions, and structure your video with a clear beginning, middle, and end. This creates a narrative flow that keeps viewers engaged.

- **Enhancing Engagement:** Raw footage can be shaky, have unwanted background noise, or lack visual appeal. Editing software allows you to:
  1. **Stabilize shaky footage:** Ensure smooth, professional-looking visuals.
  2. **Fix audio issues:** Remove background noise, adjust volume levels, and even add music and sound effects to enhance the mood.
  3. **Improve visuals:** Apply colour correction, add text overlays, and incorporate transitions between scenes to create a polished look.

- **Controlling the Pacing:** Editing software lets you control the speed of your video. You can trim out unnecessary pauses, shorten lengthy scenes, or even use slow-motion and time-lapse effects to emphasize specific moments. This keeps viewers engaged and ensures your message is delivered effectively.

- **Versatility for Different Audiences:** The same raw footage can be edited into different videos depending on the target audience. Social media might require shorter, fast-paced videos, while a corporate presentation might benefit from a more detailed and informative style. Editing software empowers you to tailor your video for its specific purpose.

In short, video editing software takes your raw video and transforms it into a powerful communication tool, allowing you to tell a story, inform, entertain, or persuade your audience.

CHAPTER TWO
Getting Started

Installation and Setup

Adobe Premiere Pro offers a plethora of editing tools and presets that empower video creators to achieve diverse visual effects effortlessly.

Its user-friendly interface is particularly advantageous for newcomers, enabling them to utilize its features effectively from the outset. If you're seeking a video editing application that excels in producing outstanding visual content, Adobe Premiere Pro is an ideal selection.

Below are the steps to download and install Adobe Premiere Pro on your device:

1. **Visit the official Adobe website:** Go to the Adobe website using your preferred web browser.

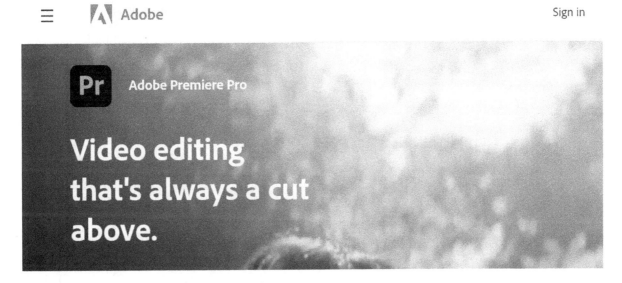

2. **Navigate to the Premiere Pro page:** Locate the Premiere Pro product page within the Adobe Creative Cloud suite.

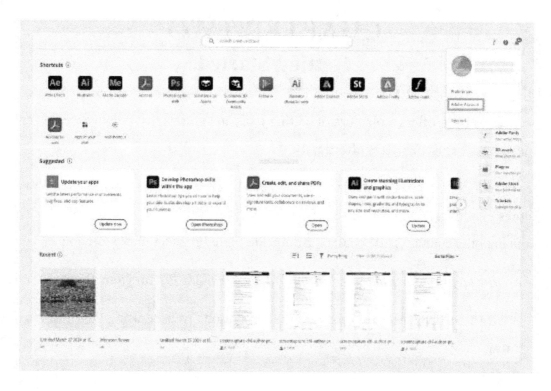

3. **Choose your subscription plan:** Adobe offers various subscription plans tailored to different user needs. Select the plan that best fits your requirements and budget.

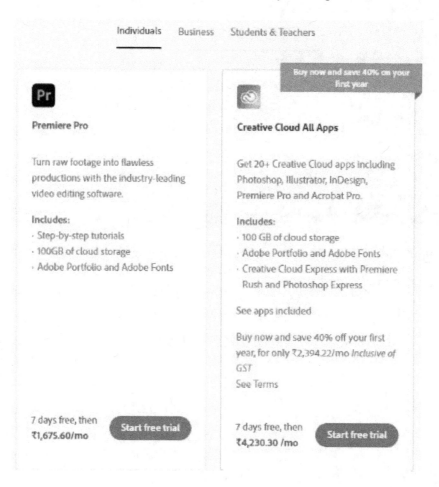

4. **Sign in or create an Adobe ID:** If you don't already have an Adobe ID, you'll need to create one to proceed with the download and installation process.

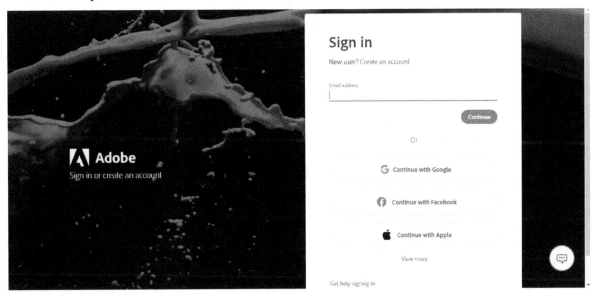

5. **Download Adobe Creative Cloud:** Before you can access Premiere Pro, you'll need to download and install the Adobe Creative Cloud desktop application. This serves as a hub for managing all your Adobe software subscriptions.

6. **Install Premiere Pro:** Once Creative Cloud is installed, you can access Premiere Pro from the application's interface. Click on the Premiere Pro icon and follow the on-screen instructions to download and install the software on your device.

7. **Launch Premiere Pro:** After the installation is complete, launch Adobe Premiere Pro from the Creative Cloud desktop application or your device's applications folder.

8. **Sign in and start editing:** Upon launching Premiere Pro, sign in with your Adobe ID credentials. Once logged in, you're ready to start creating and editing videos using Adobe Premiere Pro's powerful suite of tools and features.

By following these steps, you can easily download and install Adobe Premiere Pro on your device and begin creating stunning visual content with ease.

Interface Overview

The Premiere interface displayed below is cantered on the Editing Workspace. To switch to a different Workspace, follow these steps:

- Navigate to the menu bar at the top of the Premiere Pro interface.
- Click on "Window" to reveal a drop-down menu.
- From the drop-down menu, select "Workspaces."
- In the submenu that appears, choose "Editing."

Alternatively, you can directly select the Editing tab from the Workspaces options displayed at the top of the interface. This method offers a quick way to switch between different predefined workspaces tailored to specific editing tasks, such as Colour, Effects, or Audio.

Here's some additional information on each element of the Premiere interface in the Editing Workspace:

- **Menu bar**: The menu bar provides access to various options for managing projects, editing tools, and interface preferences. Under the File menu, users can find options for creating, saving, and exporting projects. The Window menu allows customization of the interface by toggling panels on or off.

- **Workspace Tabs**: Premiere Pro offers several predefined workspaces tailored to different editing tasks, such as Editing, Color, Effects, and Audio. Users can switch between these workspaces to optimize the layout and toolsets for their specific workflow.

- **Source Monitor**: The Source Monitor allows users to preview and scrub through footage before adding it to the project timeline. It provides essential playback controls and displays information about the selected clip, such as resolution, frame rate, and duration.

- **Program panel**: This panel displays the edited project as it will appear to viewers. Users can review their edits, transitions, effects, and audio levels in real-time. The Program panel also provides playback controls and options for adjusting the viewing resolution.

- **Project panel**: The Project panel serves as the central hub for managing media assets within a project. Users can import video, audio, images, and graphics into the project, organize them into folders (bins), and perform tasks like renaming, sorting, and searching for assets.

- **Toolbar**: The Toolbar contains a comprehensive set of tools for editing and manipulating media within the project. Tools such as Selection, Razor, Pen, and Hand are commonly used for basic editing tasks like cutting, trimming, and adding effects to clips.

- **Timeline**: The Timeline is where the majority of editing work takes place. Users arrange and sequence clips, apply effects and transitions, adjust audio levels, and create complex edits using layers and keyframes. The Timeline provides a visual representation of the project's structure over time.

- **Audio Meter**: The Audio Meter provides visual feedback on the volume levels of audio tracks in the Timeline. It helps users monitor audio levels to ensure proper mixing and prevent clipping or distortion during playback and export.

By understanding and utilizing these elements effectively, users can streamline their editing workflow and create professional-quality videos with Adobe Premiere Pro.

Workspaces in Premiere Pro define the layout of the interface, comprising various windows and panels. Depending on the chosen Workspace, the arrangement of panels and overall appearance of Premiere Pro will adjust accordingly.

Several Workspace presets are available by default and can be accessed through the Interface Menu. The Editing Workspace is commonly preferred for most editing tasks. However, panels can be rearranged and resized with a simple click-and-drag action, sometimes unintentionally.

If any changes occur, such as resizing or removing a panel, the Workspace can easily be restored to its default settings.

To reset the Workspace layout, follow these steps: Go to Window > Workspace > Reset to Saved Layout.

Using Panels:

To access a panel that is not currently visible, navigate to Window in the Menu Bar and select the desired panel. Panels with a checkmark to the left are currently accessible from the main interface.

To expand a panel, allowing access to additional tabs, click the double-arrows located at the top of the panel.

For further options, such as closing or undocking a panel, click the three stacked lines near the panel or tab name. This menu allows users to customize their workspace according to their preferences.

Project Settings

Project settings in Adobe Premiere Elements define the characteristics of your video and audio assets within a project. These settings include parameters like format (e.g., AVCHD), source (e.g., hard disk or Flash memory camcorder), aspect ratio (standard or widescreen), frame rate, audio sample rate, upper or lower field first, and bit depth.

When initiating a new project, Adobe Premiere Elements automatically applies a project preset, which consists of preconfigured project settings. By default, the project preset aligns with the television standard corresponding to the installed version of Adobe Premiere Elements on your computer.

NTSC (National Television Standards Committee) serves as the television standard for regions including the Americas, the Caribbean, Japan, South Korea, and Taiwan.

PAL (Phase Alternating Line) stands as the standard format utilized in Europe, Russia, Africa, the Middle East, India, Australia, New Zealand, the South Pacific, China, and other parts of Asia.

It's crucial to verify the format of your source footage before selecting a project preset since you cannot modify the project preset once the project is initiated. Ensuring compatibility between the project preset and source footage format is essential for smooth editing and optimal output quality.

Dynamic sequence preset

When you insert a movie clip into the Expert view timeline in Adobe Premiere Elements, the software dynamically adjusts your project settings behind the scenes to align with the properties of the clip.

These properties encompass dimensions, frame rate (fps), pixel aspect ratio, and field order. This dynamic adjustment ensures that your project settings seamlessly match the specifications of the inserted clip, enabling smoother editing and maintaining optimal quality throughout your editing process.

Select presets and change settings

Adobe Premiere Elements provides default project presets tailored for various common media sources such as cameras, DVD discs, and mobile phones, among others.

While you can choose from a range of available presets, the software doesn't support the creation of custom presets. The presets for a project must be selected during the project creation process, and they cannot be modified afterward.

The Project Presets are conveniently listed in the New Project dialog box. To access a comprehensive list of all presets along with their settings, you can select "More" and then click on "View All Presets." This feature enables users to easily identify and select the most suitable preset for their specific project requirements.

To select a project preset in Adobe Premiere Elements, follow these steps:

1. Launch Adobe Premiere Elements.
2. In the Home screen, click on "Video Editor," then select "New Project." Alternatively, you can choose "File" > "New" > "Project."
3. You'll be presented with a list of available presets categorized by Landscape, Portrait, Square, and Social. You can also click on "More" and then "View All Presets" to access additional presets categorized by Aspect Ratio or Video Standard.
4. Review the available presets and select the one that matches the format, television standard, and aspect ratio of the footage you intend to edit.
5. Once you've selected the desired preset, click "OK."
6. Provide a name and choose a location for your project files, then click "OK" to create the project.

By following these steps, you can select the appropriate project preset in Adobe Premiere Elements, ensuring that your project settings align with the specifications of your footage for smooth editing and optimal results.

Once you've created a project in Adobe Premiere Elements, you can only make minor display-related adjustments to the project settings.

Here's how to do it:

1. Open your project in Adobe Premiere Elements.
2. Go to the menu bar and choose "Edit" > "Project Settings" > "General."
3. In the Project Settings dialog box, you can specify settings for General, Capture, and Video Rendering according to your requirements.
4. Make the desired changes to the project settings.
5. Once you've adjusted the settings, click "OK" to apply the changes.

By following these steps, you can modify the project settings for an existing project in Adobe Premiere Elements. However, please note that the changes you can make are limited to minor display-related adjustments.

General settings

General settings (Edit > Project Settings > General) govern the essential properties of a project. They include the video processing mode, frame size, aspect ratios, count time (Display Format), and playback settings (Timebase).

These parameters correspond to the most popular source media in your project. For example, if the majority of your film is DV, select the DV Playback editing mode.

If you alter these settings at random, the quality of your video may suffer. The general settings comprise the following choices.

1. **Editing Mode:** Determines the television standard and format for the project, such as PAL or NTSC. This setting is fixed and cannot be changed after the project is created.

2. **Timebase:** Specifies the time divisions used for calculating the time position of each edit. PAL uses 25 frames per second (fps), while NTSC uses 29.97 fps.

3. **Playback Settings:** Controls where previews will play in the DV editing mode. This option is available if using a DV preset or plug-in with additional playback functions.

4. **Frame Size:** Defines the frame dimensions for project playback, usually matching the frame size of the source media. Adjusting playback settings can be done by right-clicking or ctrl-clicking the monitor and selecting Playback Settings.

5. **Pixel Aspect Ratio:** Sets the aspect ratio for pixels based on the video format (PAL or NTSC). Mismatching this ratio with your video format can cause distortion during rendering and playback.

6. **Fields:** Specifies the field dominance, indicating the order in which the interlaced fields of each frame are drawn.

7. **Display Format (video):** Determines how time is displayed throughout the project, corresponding to standards for editing video and motion-picture film. For example, choose 30-fps Drop-Frame Timecode for DV NTSC video and 25-fps Timecode for DV PAL video.

8. **Title Safe Area:** Marks a safe zone for titles to prevent them from being cut off by TVs that zoom the picture.

9. **Action Safe Area:** Marks a safe zone for action to ensure it's not excluded by TVs that zoom the picture.

10. **Sample Rate:** Identifies the audio sample rate for the project preset. Higher rates offer better audio quality but require more disk space and processing.

11. **Display Format (audio):** Specifies whether audio time display is measured in audio samples or milliseconds, providing precision for audio editing tasks.

It's important to understand these settings as they affect the quality and compatibility of your project. Making informed choices during project setup ensures smooth editing and optimal output quality.

CHAPTER THREE
Importing Media

Importing Files and Folders

Adobe Premiere has several methods for importing media files. To import media, use the File menu (⌘I) or navigate to its location in the Media Browser.

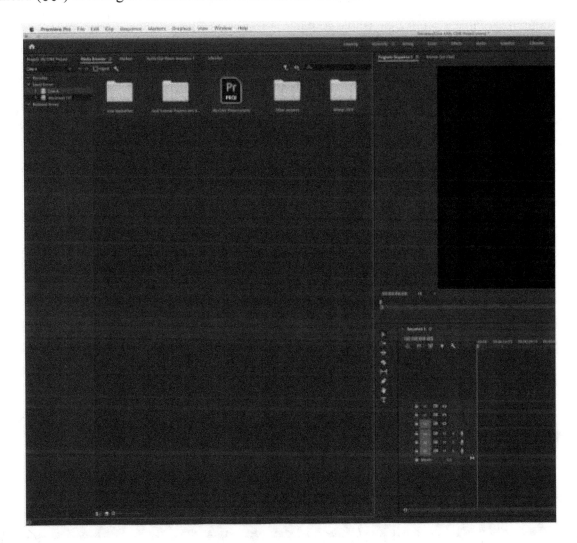

If your media files are already stored on an external hard drive, you have two options to import them into Premiere. The files will remain in their original location on the hard drive but will be accessible through the Project tab in Premiere.

If your media files are still on your camera or SD card, it's crucial to copy them over to your external hard drive first. Depending on your camera type and recording settings, your files may be located on the top level of the card as .mp4 or .mov files, or within a Private folder.

Regardless of their location, it's best practice to copy the entire contents of the SD card to an external hard drive before importing. We recommend creating a dedicated folder on your hard drive with a descriptive and unique name to avoid losing track of your media. For more guidance on managing media from SD cards effectively, refer to this page on workflow for file management.

Once your media is copied over, you can proceed with the import process as usual.

After importing, the files will appear in the Project tab (typically located on the left-hand side). To maintain organization, it's advisable to rename imported files with specific names for easy identification.

Additionally, consider creating folders (referred to as Bins in Premiere) to further organize your media based on parameters like shoot date, media type, or quality. This systematic approach ensures efficient project management and helps you stay focused on your creative process.

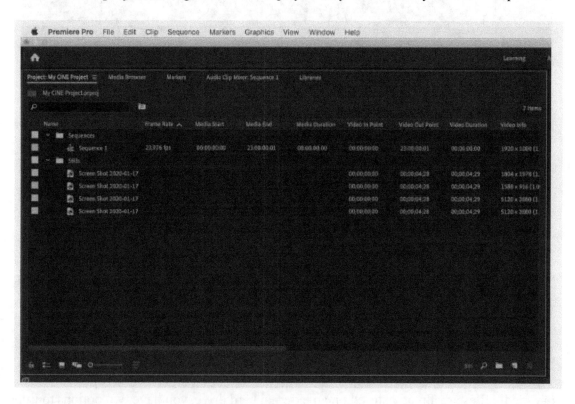

Advanced Selection and Review Tools

Here's a quick overview of other approaches and tools you can use to review and select material.

Bins: Bins are essential organizational tools in Premiere Pro for storing and managing all media and assets, including sequences, within the Project window. They serve various purposes, with some of the most important being:

1. **Organizing by Media Type:** Bins can be created to categorize media files based on their type, such as video clips, audio files, images, etc.
2. **Organizing by Scene or Character:** Bins can also be used to organize media files based on scenes, characters, locations, or any other relevant criteria for your project.

In and Out Points: In and out points allow you to select specific sections of a clip to bring down to your Sequence or to create subclips for further organization within your bins.

Sub Clips: Sub clips are smaller sections extracted from larger clips and can be independently organized within bins. They are created by selecting a range from a clip in the Source Viewer using in and out points and then creating a sub clip from the Clip Menu. Sub clips are particularly useful when dealing with long master clips like interviews.

Markers: Markers can be added to clips in the Source Viewer or Timeline to tag specific frames or clips with notes. This feature is helpful for adding additional information about a clip or marking areas that need attention or editing.

Search Bins: Search bins are dynamic bins created in the Project Window by clicking on the folder icon with a magnifying glass. These bins automatically update to match specified criteria, making them useful for quickly accessing specific types of media. For example, you can create a search bin that contains all close-up shots or all shots of a particular character by adding notes or descriptions to clips and then searching for them using the search function.

By utilizing these organizational features effectively, you can streamline your workflow, improve project management, and quickly access the media assets you need for editing.

Supported File Formats

Some filename extensions, such as MOV, AVI, and MXF, represent container file formats rather than specific audio, video, or image data formats. Container files can store data encoded with a variety of compression and encoding algorithms.

Premiere Pro can import these container files, but the ability to import the data within them is dependent on the codecs (particularly, decoders) loaded.

Supported sequence, still image, and movie sizes

Sequence Size

Video and still-image files you intend to import must not exceed the maximum dimensions allowed. The maximum sequence frame size is 10,240×8,192 pixels (width x height). If you try to set a Frame Size dimension higher than this limit in the Sequence Settings dialog box, Premiere Pro resets the value to the maximum.

Still image and movie sizes

The maximum frame size for importing still photographs and movies is 256 megapixels, with a maximum dimension of 32,768 pixels in each direction. Images with dimensions of 16,000×16,000 pixels and 32,000×8,000 pixels are okay, however 35,000×10,000 pixels are not.

Premiere Pro allows you to import and work with a wide range of video, audio, and image formats.

Here's a breakdown of some of the most common ones:

Video:

High-Quality Formats:

- Apple ProRes: A widely used format for acquisition, editing, and delivery, known for its excellent quality. Premiere Pro offers extensive support for ProRes workflows.
- AVC-Intra: A high-quality codec from Panasonic.
- DNxHD/HR: Professional editing formats with various compression levels.
- RAW Formats: Premiere supports RAW formats from various camera manufacturers like Canon Cinema RAW Light (CRM) and RED R3D.

Common Video Formats:

- MP4, MOV, AVI: Popular container formats that can hold different video codecs.
- H.264 AVC, HEVC (H.265): Widely used video compression formats.
- M2TS, MTS: Formats commonly used for Blu-ray and AVCHD video.
- MPEG-1, MPEG-2, MPEG-4: Established video compression standards.

- MXF: A versatile container format that supports various video codecs including AVC-Intra, DVCPRO, and XAVC.

Other Supported Formats:

- GIF: Animated images.
- HEIF: A newer image format with improved compression. (Requires additional installation on Windows)
- JPEG2000: Another image format with high compression capabilities.
- OpenEXR: High-dynamic-range image format used in visual effects.

<u>Audio:</u>

Common Audio Formats:

- AAC, MP3: Widely used compressed audio formats.
- WAV: Uncompressed audio format for high-quality applications.
- M4A: Audio format often used in MP4 container files.

Other:

Project Files:

- CRM (Canon Cinema RAW Light project files)
- Rush (Projects from Premiere Rush)

Container Formats:

- 3GP, 3G2: Multimedia container formats often used for mobile video.
- ASF (Windows only): Used for streaming media.
- VOB: Container format for DVD media.

Note: This is not an exhaustive list. Premiere Pro supports many other formats. Additionally, some formats may require specific codecs to be installed on your system for proper playback.

Supported still-image and still-image sequence file formats

Premiere Pro allows you to import and use various image formats in your video projects. Here are some of the most common ones:

Graphic Design Formats:
- AI, EPS: Vector graphics formats from Adobe Illustrator, perfect for logos and sharp-edged graphics that won't lose quality when resized.
- PSD: Photoshop Document format, which can contain layers, effects, and other editing information.

Raster Image Formats:
- BMP, DIB, RLE: These formats are generally large and uncompressed, suitable for simple graphics.
- DPX: A high-quality image format commonly used in film and digital cinema.
- GIF: Animated image format for creating short, looping animations.
- ICO: Icon files specifically used on Windows for representing applications and files.
- JPEG, JPG, JFIF: The most common image format, good for photos but with some quality loss due to compression.
- PNG: Portable Network Graphics format, known for its sharp quality and support for transparency (useful for logos with clear backgrounds).
- TGA: A versatile image format often used in video game development and texture creation.
- TIFF: Tagged Interchange File format, a high-quality format suitable for professional printing and archiving.

Premiere Pro supports closed captioning and subtitle files in several formats, allowing you to add text overlays that synchronize with the audio in your video.

Here's a breakdown of each format:

- **DFXP (Distribution Format Exchange Profile):** A widely used exchange format for closed captions, compatible with various broadcast and playback systems.
- **MCC (MacCaption VANC):** A format for closed captions specifically designed for MacCaption software and utilizes Vertical Analog Control (VANC) data channels.
- **SCC (Scenarist Closed Caption File):** A format created by Scenarist software, commonly used in the film and video production industry.

- **SRT (SubRip Subtitle format):** A simple, human-readable text file format for subtitles, popular due to its ease of use and editing.
- **STL (EBU N19 Subtitle File):** A format based on the EBU N19 standard, used for subtitles in European broadcast television.
- **XML (W3C/SMPTE/EBU Timed Text File):** An XML-based format for timed text, offering flexibility for advanced styling and effects.

Here's a breakdown of the video project file formats supported by Premiere Pro:

Project Interchange:
- **AAF (Advanced Authoring Format):** A universal format for exchanging project information between different editing software applications.
- **FCP XML (Final Cut Pro XML):** Allows importing project data from Final Cut Pro, another video editing program.

Premiere Pro Specific Projects:
- **PRPROJ:** The native project file format for Premiere Pro. Use this to save and reopen your editing projects within Premiere Pro.
- **PREL (Windows only):** Project files created by Adobe Premiere Elements, a more consumer-oriented video editing application by Adobe. (Limited support on Windows only)

Other Project Types:
- **AEP, AEPX (After Effects project):** While not strictly video editing projects, Premiere Pro can import After Effects projects containing animations, motion graphics, and visual effects that can be incorporated into your video.
- **CHPROJ (Character Animator Project):** Similar to After Effects projects, Premiere Pro can import Character Animator projects which allow you to integrate animated characters into your video.
- **CSV, PBL, TXT, TAB (Batch Lists):** These text-based file formats can be used to create lists of files or clips for import into Premiere Pro, streamlining your workflow.
- **EDL (Edit Decision List):** A text file format containing edit instructions, often used for exchanging editing information between different editing systems. (Limited support, specific format - CMX3600 EDLs)

Preserve audio sync for variable frame rate footage

You can use variable frame footage from devices like mobile phones and DJI Phantoms without having to manually change the audio-video sync.

- Choose a VFR clip from the Project panel or the Source Monitor, then choose Master Clip Effect in the Effect Controls panel.
- Toggle between the options below:

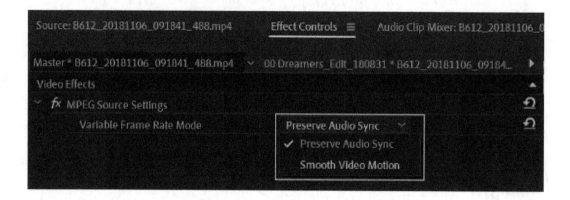

- **Preserve Audio Sync:** This feature ensures that the audio and video remain synchronized by adjusting the frame rate. It achieves this by either adding or dropping frames, which may lead to a choppier visual appearance. Preserve Audio Sync is automatically applied to all Variable Frame Rate (VFR) clips with audio.
- **Smooth Video Motion:** This option decodes all frames from the source without prioritizing audio-video synchronization. It results in smoother motion in the video but may lead to audio-video discrepancies. Smooth Video Motion is the default setting when Premiere Pro does not detect audio in VFR clips. It's ideal for motion graphics work where obtaining all available video frames is prioritized over maintaining audio-video sync.

Limitations for variable frame rate support

If you intend to use proxy, consolidation, or transcoding procedures, it is preferable to convert VFR footage to a consistent frame rate before editing. If you manually synced VFR footage in a prior version of Premiere Pro, resync it when you open the project in 12.0.1 or later.

Organizing Media in the Project Panel

The Project panel allows you to utilize bins to organize project items in the same manner as folders do in Windows

Explorer or the macOS Finder. Bins may include source files, sequences, or other bins. As your project grows, you can create more bins to hold the things. While creating and using bins is optional (especially for short-form projects), they are quite handy for organizing your project files.

Bins can be used in the following ways:

- Store offline clips for batch capture.
- To store both main and backup sequences.
- To categorize files by kind, such as video, still photos, and audio.

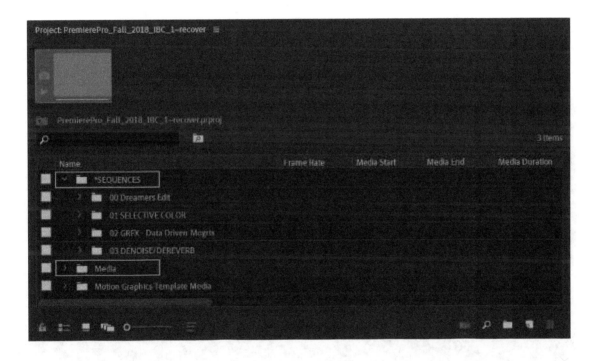

The default behaviours of bins in the Project panel are as follows. The final three bin default behaviours can be changed by going to general settings and editing bin behaviour.

Organize bins.

You can sort and examine bins in the Project panel using the following methods:

- **List view**: All bins are displayed vertically in a scrollable list. Clicking the arrow opens the bins, allowing you to examine the files inside.

- **Icon view:** All bins are organized horizontally in folders. To view the contents of a folder, simply click on it. This view shows you exactly what type of file is in the bin.
- **Freeform view:** This view lets you to organize your bins and files in any way that suits you.

Creating, removing, and opening bins

- To create a bin, click the New Bin button at the bottom of the Project screen. You can also use the keyboard shortcuts Control+/ (Windows) and Command+/ (Mac OS).
- To delete one or more bins, select them and then click the Delete symbol toward the bottom of the Project panel. You can also remove bins by selecting one or more and pressing the Delete key.
- Double-click to open a bin's dockable panel.

Change bin behaviours

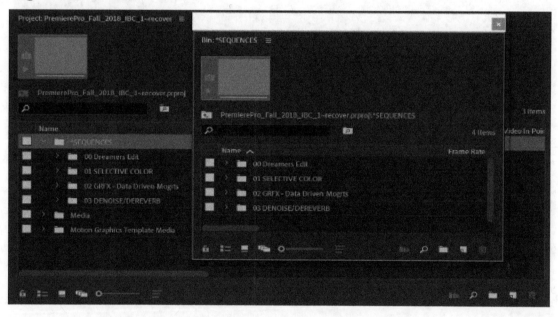

While working on a project, you may want to reconsider how you approach your bins. The basic layout allows you to examine the hierarchy of your entire project, which is useful. However, you may want to open a bin in a separate tab or in a different panel. This allows you to focus on clips in a certain bin, arrange clips in storyboard order in icon mode, or search for clips within a bin by typing into the search bar. Some editors prefer to have the bin window overlap the interface, but others prefer to have bins open in place or in other tabs.

To open a bin in its own floating panel, in situ, or in a new tab, perform the following:

- Double-clicking a bin will open it in a new tab. This panel can be docked or grouped with any other panel.

- To open a bin in place, use Ctrl-double-click (Windows) or Command-double-click (Mac OS).

- To open a bin in its own floating panel, use Alt-double-click (Windows) or Option-double-click (MacOS).

You can modify the default behaviours of Project panel bins by modifying the Bins options.

- Choose Edit > Preferences > General (Windows) or Premiere Pro > Preferences > General (Mac OS).

- In the Bins area, choose options from the menus for double-click, + Ctrl (Windows) or + Command (macOS), and + Alt (Windows) or + Opt (macOS).

- Select "OK."

Label assets

Labels are colours used to identify and associate assets. You can apply and view labels in the Project panel. Label colours are used to identify assets in the Project panel's Label column as well as in the Timeline panel.

- To give a label to an asset, choose a clip from the Project panel, then Edit > Label and select a colour.

- To pick all assets with the same label, choose one object with the label and then click Edit > Label > pick Label Group.

- To change label names or colours, select Edit > Preferences > Label Colours (Windows) or Premiere Pro > Preferences > Label Colours (macOS). To change a colour, select a colour swatch.

- To set default labels for a media type, select Edit > Preferences > Label Defaults (Windows) or Premiere Pro > Preferences > Label Defaults (macOS).

CHAPTER FOUR
Editing Basics

Timeline Basics

The timeline is the heart of editing in Adobe Premiere Pro.

Here's a breakdown of the timeline basics:

The Timeline Interface:

Tracks: The timeline is divided into horizontal tracks. Each track can hold a video clip, audio clip, image, or title. You can add more tracks as needed for your project. Tracks can be added to the Timeline to create layers for grading, audio, and framing adjustments (pan and scan).

Multiple tracks

You can include the following music in the Timeline:

- Footage: Blue track. To add footage into the timeline
- Grading: Red track. To add a grading track number
- Audio: solid green track. To add an audio track, open the Desktop, find the audio file (wav or aiff), and drag it to the Timeline. Repeat the technique with additional audio files. To adjust sound output parameters, such as the mixing frequency, go to Settings > Sound. The Settings option is located in the upper-right area of the SpeedGrade workspace.

Pan and scan: Transparent green track. To include a pan and scan track.

Manage tracks

The Timeline's tracks can be managed using the tools on the left side of each track.

Drag, lock, and eye icons

- To reveal or hide the track, select the Eye icon.
- To lock or unlock a track, click the Lock symbol.
- To delete a track, click the Drag symbol and drag it from the Timeline.

Clips: Video clips, audio clips, and other media elements you import into your project appear as blocks on the timeline. You can drag and drop clips onto tracks to arrange them in your desired order.

Playhead: A vertical line on the timeline that indicates the current playback position in your project. The playhead displays a frame in the Monitor at any point along the Timeline. Drag the playhead to move it through the timeline.

Playhead controller

Note: To view more than one frame at a time, create additional playheads. Multiple playheads are useful for comparing different parts of the same shot or scene.

Timeline Controls: Buttons at the bottom of the timeline allow you to play, pause, rewind, and fast forward your project. You can also adjust the playback speed here.

Play a section of the timeline.

Repositioning in- and out-points allows you to specify which part of the Timeline to play. The two points are situated above the tracks, at each end of the video or playlist.

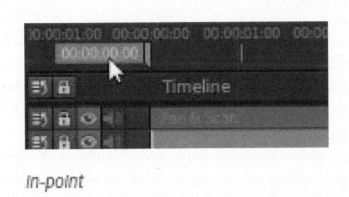

In-point

To reposition the in- and out-points, you can do the following:

- Drag the in and out points along the timeline.
- Hold Shift and drag two points together.
- Control-click the in- or out-point to return it to its original location.
- Double-click a clip to set its start and end positions. Double-click again to set the timeline's start and end points.

Navigate along the Timeline

When you have a busy timeline with multiple clips and tracks, here's how to quickly navigate around:

Move between clips:
- **Windows:** Use **Ctrl+Shift+Right Arrow** to jump to the next clip and **Ctrl+Shift+Left Arrow** for the previous clip.
- **Mac:** Use **Cmd+Shift+Right Arrow** to go to the next clip and **Cmd+Shift+Left Arrow** for the previous one.

Switch between tracks:

- Both Windows and Mac: Use **Ctrl/Cmd + Shift + Up Arrow** to move to the track above and **Ctrl/Cmd + Shift + Down Arrow** to move to the track below.

Basic Editing Techniques:

- **Trimming clips:** Drag the edges of a clip on the timeline to shorten it. You can trim from the beginning, end, or both sides.
- **Cutting clips:** Click at a specific point on a clip to split it into two separate clips. You can then delete unwanted sections or rearrange the clips.
- **Arranging clips:** Drag and drop clips on the timeline to change their order and structure your video.
- **Adding transitions:** Transitions are short effects used between clips to create a smooth flow. Premiere Pro offers various transition options.

Working with Layers:

- You can stack clips on top of each other on different tracks to create layered effects. For example, you can place a video clip on the bottom track and an audio clip on the track above it.
- You can adjust the opacity of clips to control their transparency, allowing elements from lower tracks to show through.

Essential Keyboard Shortcuts:

- **Spacebar:** Play/Pause playback
- **Left/Right Arrow Keys:** Move the playhead one frame at a time
- **I/O Keys:** Set In and Out points to mark a specific section for editing (I = In point, O = Out point)
- **Delete Key:** Delete the selected clip or section
- **Ctrl/Cmd + Z:** Undo the last edit action

Tips for Working with the Timeline:

- **Use the Zoom tool:** Zoom in and out of the timeline to see clip details or get a broader overview of your project.

- **Enable snapping:** Snapping helps clips and edits align precisely on the timeline for cleaner cuts and transitions.
- **Name your clips:** Give clear names to your clips for better organization in the timeline and project panel.
- **Colour code your tracks:** Assign different colours to your video, audio, and graphics tracks for easier visual identification.

By understanding these basic concepts, you can effectively use the timeline in Premiere Pro to arrange and edit your video clips, building your video projects from start to finish.

Cutting, Trimming, and Splitting Clips

Splitting a clip generates a new, independent instance of the original clip. The resulting clip is a tweaked version of the original, with different In and Out points.

Cut clips using the Razor tool.

- Drag the clip you want to split to the Timeline.
- Select the Razor tool from the panel.
- Click on the clip where you wish to make the split.

To divide only the audio or video section of linked clips, use Alt-click (Windows) or Option-click (macOS) while working with the Razor tool.

Split clips on the targeted tracks.

- To target specific tracks, select their headers.
- Position the playhead where you wish to split the clip(s).
- Select Sequence > Add Edit, or press Ctrl + K (Windows) or Command + K (Mac OS).

To divide all clips except locked tracks, use the Timeline panel's Sequence > Add Edit to All Tracks option.

Trim

Once you've created a "rough cut" sequence on the timeline, trim clips to fine-tune the edits and timing.

- Choose which clip you want to cut.

- Hover your cursor over the edge of the clip until you see the trim icon.

- Select and drag the clip's edge to the desired clipping length.

Other trimming tools

Ripple Edit Tool.

Use the Ripple Edit Tool to trim a clip's edge and automatically close the gap with the clip next to it.

- Choose the clip you wish to edit in the timeline.

- To enable the Ripple Edit Tool, use the B key on your keyboard.

- To shorten or lengthen a clip, click and drag the end to the left or right.

Rolling Editing Tool

Use the Rolling Edit Tool to shift the cut point between two clips.

The Rolling Edit Tool allows you to change the cut point between two clips without modifying the total duration of the clips.

When you use the Rolling Edit Tool to choose an edit point, you select both sides of it. Choose the clip you wish to edit in the timeline.

To enable the Rolling Edit Tool, use the N key on your keyboard. To alter the timing, select and drag the clip's edge to the left or right.

Keyboard Shortcuts

To open the Rolling Edit Tool, press Ctrl-click (Windows) or Command-click (macOS) on the edit spot with Ripple Edit Tool. To trim only one track of a linked clip, perform a split edit (L-cut or J-cut) while holding down Alt (Windows) or Option (MacOS).

Slip Tool

Use the Slip Tool to change the In and Out points of a clip without moving it in the timeline. This type of edit is ideal for adjusting the timing of footage within a clip without changing the overall length or the position of adjacent clips in the timeline.

A slip edit moves a clip's In and Out points forward or backward by the same number of frames in one movement. By dragging with the Slip Tool, you can adjust the starting and ending frames of a clip without changing its duration or disrupting nearby clips.

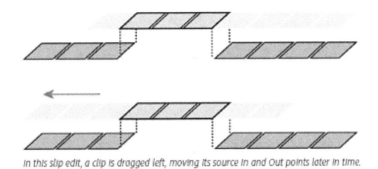

In this slip edit, a clip is dragged left, moving its source In and Out points later in time.

- Choose the clip you wish to edit in the timeline.
- To activate Slip Tool, press the Y key on your keyboard.
- Drag left or right over the footage to adjust its in and out points. The clip's overall duration will remain the same.

Keyboard Shortcuts

Action	Windows Shortcut	macOS Shortcut
Slip selection left by 5 frames	Ctrl + Alt + Shift + Left Arrow	Option + Shift + Command + Left Arrow
Slip selection left by 1 frame	Alt + Shift + Left Arrow	Option + Command + Left Arrow
Slip selection right by 5 frames	Ctrl + Alt + Shift + Right Arrow	Option + Shift + Command + Right Arrow

Slip selection right by 1 frame	Alt + Shift + Right Arrow	Option + Command + Right Arrow

Slide Tool

Use the Slide Tool to modify the location of a clip in the timeline without affecting its in and out points.

A slide edit moves a clip in time while editing nearby clips to compensate for the change. When you drag a clip left or right with the Slide Tool, the out point of the previous clip and the in point of the next clip are reduced by the number of frames you move the clip. The clip's In and Out points (and thus its runtime) remain constant.

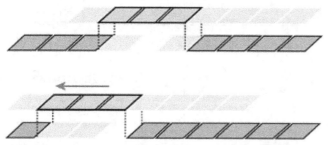

In this slide edit, a clip is dragged left to start earlier in the sequence, shortening the preceding clip and lengthening the following clip.

- Choose the clip you wish to edit in the timeline.
- To activate Slide Tool, press the U key on your keyboard.
- To move the clip to a new location in the timeline, simply click and drag it left or right.

Keyboard shortcut

Action	Windows Shortcut	macOS Shortcut
Slide selection left by 5 frames	Alt + Shift + Comma (,)	Option + Shift + Comma (,)
Slide selection left by 1 frame	Alt + Comma (,)	Option + Comma (,)
Slide selection right by 5 frames	Alt + Shift + Period (.)	Option + Shift + Period (.)
Slide selection right by 1 frame	Alt + Period (.)	Option + Period (.)

Adding and Adjusting Transitions

A transition is an effect used to create an animated link between two pieces of material. Transitions are used to transfer a scene from one shot to another. Premiere Pro includes a list of transitions that can be applied to a sequence. Transitions might be subtle crossfades or sophisticated effects.

Premiere Pro offers the following transitions:

1. Audio transitions
2. Video transitions
3. VR transitions.

By default, inserting one clip next to another in a Timeline panel causes a cut, with the last frame of one clip followed by the beginning frame of the next.

Transitions are typically situated along a cut line between shots. You can also use a transition only at the start or finish of a clip.

Trim the clips first, then apply the transition. Then use the transition.

The more you trim, the more frames you'll have available for use in the transition.

TIP: To get a cantered 1:00 transition, trim at least 15 frames from each clip.

Apply transitions between two clips.

To add a transition between two clips (cantered on the cut line), they must be on the same track and have no space between them.

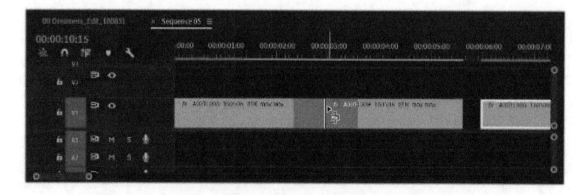

To create a transition between two clips, perform the following:

- Select Window > Effects.
- Expand the Video Transitions or Audio Transitions bins.
- Expand the bin holding the transition you intend to utilize.
- Drag the transition to the cut line between two clips, then release the mouse when the Centre at Cut icon appears.

Use a single-sided transition.

Transitions are often double-sided since they apply to both clips. Single-sided transitions are only applied to a single clip. This is useful if you do not have a clip handle.

A double-sided transition has a dark diagonal line running across it on a Timeline panel or the Effect Controls panel, whereas a single-sided transition is divided diagonally into one half dark and one half bright.

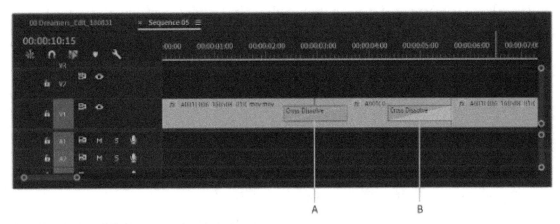

Difference between a single-sided and double-sided transition

A. Double-sided transition B. Single-sided transitions

To use a single-sided transition, perform the following:

- In the Effects panel, locate the transition you wish to use. Expand the Video Transitions or Audio Transitions bins. Then, expand the bin holding the transition you intend to use.
- To add a transition to a single cut, drag it into the Timeline panel using Ctrl+drag (Windows) or Cmd+drag (Mac OS). When you see the End At Cut or Start At Cut icons, release the mouse button.
1. End At Cut icon: Sets the transition's end point to match the conclusion of the first clip.
2. Start At Cut icon: symbol aligns the beginning of the transition with the beginning of the second clip.

Set a default transition.

- Select Window > Effects and then expand the Video Transitions or Audio Transitions bin.
- Choose the transition you want to set as the default.
- Click the Effects panel's Menu button, or right-click the transition.

44

- Select Set Selected As Default Transition.

Set the duration of the default transition.

Do any of the following:

- Select Edit > Preferences > Timeline (Windows) or Premiere Pro > Preferences > Timeline (Mac OS).
- Select the Effects panel menu button. Select Set Default Transition Duration.
- Change the value of the Video Transition Default Duration or Audio Transition Default Duration, then click OK.

Show transitions in the Effect Controls panel.

The Effect Controls panel allows you to adjust the settings for a transition that you've placed in a sequence. Transition parameters varies for each transition.

In the Effect Controls panel, the adjacent clips and transitions are shown in A-roll/B-roll mode.

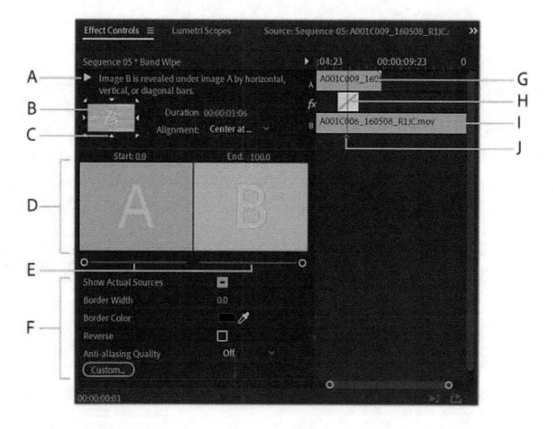

A. Play The Transition button

B. Transition preview

C. Edge selector

D. Clip previews

E. Start and End sliders

F. Transition settings

G. Clip A (first clip)

H. Transition

I. Clip B (second clip)

J. Current-time indicator

- To open the Effects control panel, select the transition from the Timeline panel.
- To preview the transition in the Effect Controls window, click the Play the Transition button. The program monitor is unaffected by this.
- Select the Show Actual Sources checkbox in the Effect Controls panel to see frames from the actual clip or clips.

Align a transition within the Timeline panel.

- To align a transition in the Timeline panel, perform the following:

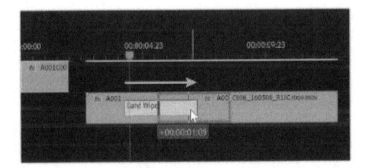

- Zoom in on the Timeline tab to observe the transition more clearly.
- Move the transition over the cut to relocate it.

Align a transition with the Effect Controls panel.

To open a transition in the Effect Controls panel, choose it in the Timeline panel.

Do any of the following:

- Select an option from the Alignment menu.

Centre At Cut or Custom Start: The transition's starting and ending points move in opposite directions.

Start At Cut: Only the last part of the transition moves.

End At Cut: Only the start of the transition moves.

- Position the pointer in the Effect Controls time ruler over the transition's centre until the Slide Transition icon appears. Drag the transition as desired. Magnify the time ruler to provide finer control.

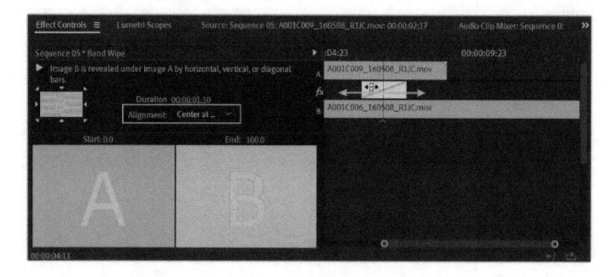

CHAPTER FIVE
Working with Effects

<u>Applying Video Effects</u>

Premiere Pro boasts a vast collection of video effects that can enhance your edits, add creative flair, and correct visual imperfections.

Here's a breakdown of the process for applying video effects:

The Effects Panel:
- The Effects panel in Premiere Pro houses a comprehensive library of video effects, categorized for easy browsing.
- You can search for specific effects by name or browse through categories like Colour Correction, Distort, Stylize, and more.

Adding Effects to Clips:
- Select the clip in your timeline that you want to apply an effect to.
- Go to the Effects panel. You can find it on the left-hand side of the Premiere Pro workspace by default.

- Locate the desired effect. Use the search bar or browse through categories.
- Drag the effect from the Effects panel and drop it onto your clip in the timeline.

Alternatively, you can right-click on the clip and select "Effect" followed by browsing and choosing the desired effect.

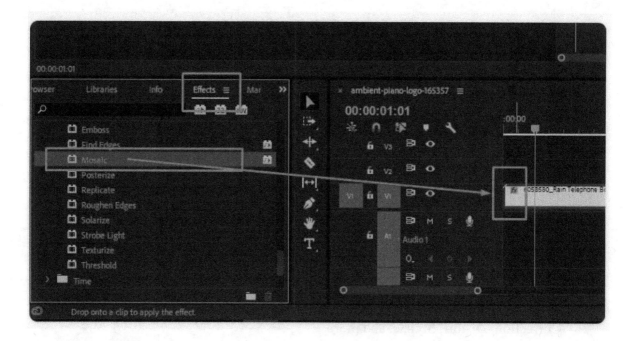

Effect Controls:

- Once applied, the effect controls will appear in the Effect Controls panel. This panel allows you to adjust the parameters of the effect and customize its appearance on your clip.

- The specific controls will vary depending on the chosen effect. Some effects might have simple on/off toggles, while others offer detailed adjustments like colour values, blur intensity, or animation settings.

Previewing and Fine-Tuning:

- Use the playback controls in your timeline to preview the effect on your clip.

- As you adjust the effect controls, the preview will update in real-time, allowing you to fine-tune the look and feel of the effect.

Removing Effects:

To remove an effect from a clip, you can either:

- Click and hold the effect in the Effects Controls panel and drag it up to the trash can icon.

- Right-click on the effect in the Effects Controls panel and select "Delete".

Tips for Working with Video Effects:
1. Experiment! Don't be afraid to try different effects and explore their capabilities.
2. Start subtle. Often, a light touch with effects is more visually appealing than overdoing them.
3. Consider your project's style. Ensure the effects you choose complement the overall tone and aesthetic of your video.
4. Use nesting for complex edits. Nest multiple clips with effects together to create a more manageable group and avoid cluttering your timeline.

By following these steps and tips, you can effectively apply video effects in Premiere Pro to elevate your video editing projects. Don't hesitate to experiment and discover the creative potential that Premiere Pro's effects offer.

Using Audio Effects

Premiere Pro's audio effects go beyond simply raising or lowering the volume. They offer a powerful toolkit for manipulating, repairing, and creatively processing the sound in your videos.

Here's how to leverage audio effects in Premiere Pro:

The Audio Effects Panel:
Similar to video effects, Premiere Pro has a dedicated **Audio Effects panel** located on the left side of the workspace by default. This panel provides access to a comprehensive library of audio effects, categorized for easy exploration.

Adding Audio Effects:
1. **Select the audio clip** in your timeline that you want to modify. This could be dialogue, music, sound effects, or any other audio element.
2. **Navigate to the Effects panel.** You can find it alongside the Video Effects panel.
3. **Locate the desired audio effect.** Browse through categories like Dynamics, EQ, Noise Reduction, or search for a specific effect by name.
4. **Drag the effect from the Audio Effects panel and drop it onto your audio clip** in the timeline.

5. Alternatively, you can right-click on the audio clip, select "Effect", and choose the desired effect from the submenu.

Effect Controls and Customization:

Once applied, the effect controls will appear in the **Effect Controls panel**. Here you can adjust the parameters of the chosen audio effect to achieve the sonic outcome you desire.

The specific controls will vary depending on the effect. For instance, an equalizer effect might offer adjustments for individual frequency bands, while a noise reduction effect might have controls for noise reduction level and spectral range.

Previewing and Making Adjustments:

- Use the playback controls in your timeline to preview how the audio effect alters your clip.
- As you tweak the effect controls in the Effect Controls panel, the preview will update in real-time, allowing you to fine-tune the sound.

Removing Audio Effects:

There are two ways to remove an audio effect from a clip:

- Drag and hold the effect in the Effects Controls panel and move it up to the trash can icon.
- Right-click on the effect in the Effects Controls panel and select "Delete".

Essential Audio Effects to Know:

- **EQ (Equalizer):** This versatile effect allows you to boost or attenuate specific frequencies in your audio, fixing imbalances or shaping the tonal quality.
- **Compressor:** Controls the dynamic range of your audio, reducing the gap between loud and quiet parts, resulting in a more consistent and controlled sound.
- **Noise Reduction:** Helps eliminate unwanted background noise like hums, hisses, or static, cleaning up your audio recordings.
- **Reverb:** Simulates the natural reflections of sound in different environments, adding depth and space to your audio.

Tips for Working with Audio Effects:
- **Listen closely.** Use high-quality headphones or monitors to accurately assess your audio and the impact of effects.
- **Subtlety is key.** Often, small adjustments with audio effects can yield significant improvements.
- **Experiment creatively.** While some effects have corrective purposes, others can be used to create unique sonic textures and stylistic enhancements.

By understanding these concepts and exploring the Audio Effects panel in Premiere Pro, you can refine and enhance the audio quality of your videos, making them more engaging and professional-sounding.

Keyframing Effects

A keyframe is the point in time at which you specify a value, such as spatial position, opacity, or audio volume. To make a change in a property over time, you must set at least two keyframes: one for the value at the start of the change and another for the value at the end of the change. Premiere Pro then does interpolation, which is a gradual shift in values between keyframes.

You can work with keyframes in either the Timeline or the Effect Controls panel.

Add keyframes.
Currently, you may add keyframes to the Timeline or the Effect Controls panel. To activate the keyframing process, select the Toggle Animation button in the Effect Controls panel.

Keyframe controls in Effect Controls panel

A. Toggle animation button B. Add/Remove keyframe button

1. In the Timeline panel, choose the clip containing the effect you want to animate.

52

2. To add and change keyframes in a Timeline panel, choose the video or audio track and make keyframes visible.

3. If the keyframes are not visible by default, click the Wrench symbol in the Timeline panel and choose Show Video Keyframes.

4. In the Effect Controls panel, click the triangle to expand the effect to which you wish to add keyframes, and then click the Toggle Animation icon to enable keyframes for an effect attribute.

5. To display the graph of the effect property, select one of the following options:

- (Effect Controls Panel) Click the triangle to expand the effect property and see the Value and Velocity graphs.

- (Timeline panel) Select an effect property from the menu adjacent to the clip or track name.

6. Move the playhead to the point in time where you wish to insert a keyframe.

7. Take one of the following actions:

- To modify the value of the effect property, click the Add/Remove Keyframe button in the Effect Controls panel.

- Use the Selection or Pen tool to Ctrl-click (Windows) or Command-click (Mac OS) a keyframe graph, and then change the value of the effect attribute. Using the Selection or Pen tool, you may add a keyframe to any location on a graph. Positioning the current-time indication is not required.

8. In order to add keyframes and modify the effect property, repeat steps 5 and 6 as necessary.

Select keyframes

A keyframe must first be selected in a Timeline panel before it can be altered or copied. Keyframes that have been chosen appear solid; those that have not are hollow. You can drag segments directly between keyframes, eliminating the need to select them beforehand.

Additionally, when you modify the keyframes that specify the ends of segments, the segments automatically reposition.

Take one of the following actions:

- Click the Keyframe icon in the Timeline panel with the Selection or Pen tools to pick a keyframe.

- Shift-click with the Selection tool or the Pen tool in a Timeline panel to choose numerous contiguous or non-contiguous keyframes.

- Draw a marquee selection box around the keyframes with the Pen tool in order to choose multiple keyframes by dragging them in the Timeline panel. To add more keyframes to an already-existing selection, shift-drag.

- Click the layer property name in the Effect Controls panel to select all keyframes for that property. To select every Position keyframe for a layer, for instance, click Position.

Delete keyframes

A keyframe can be simply removed from an effect property in the Timeline panel or the Effect Controls if it is no longer needed. Keyframes for the effect property can be deactivated or removed all at once.

When you use the Toggle Animation button in the Effect Controls to deactivate keyframes, all current keyframes are erased and cannot be created again until you reactivate them.

1. Verify that the Effect Controls panel or Timeline panel's graphs for the effect property are displayed.

2. Take one of the following actions:

- Choose Edit > Clear after selecting one or more keyframes. Another option is to hit Delete.

- Click the Add/Remove Keyframe button after navigating to the keyframe using the current time indicator.

- (Only the Effect Controls panel) Click the Toggle Animation button to the left of an effect or property name to remove all of its keyframes. Click OK to confirm your choice when asked.

View keyframes and graphs

The Effect Controls panel and Timeline panels serve distinct functions in adjusting keyframes and timing within Adobe Premiere Pro, each with its own unique approach.

The Effect Controls panel provides a comprehensive view of all effect properties, keyframes, and interpolation methods simultaneously.

Conversely, in the Timeline panel, only one effect property is displayed at a time for each clip. While the Effect Controls panel offers complete control over keyframe values, the Timeline panel provides more limited control.

For instance, adjustments involving x and y coordinates, like Position, cannot be modified directly in the Timeline panel. However, keyframe adjustments can still be made within the Timeline without needing to switch to the Effect Controls panel.

Both panels feature graphs that visualize keyframe values and the interpolated values between keyframes. A level graph indicates no change in the property value between keyframes, while an ascending or descending graph signifies an increase or decrease in the property value over time.

The speed and smoothness of property changes can be adjusted by modifying the interpolation method and manipulating Bezier curves.

By leveraging the capabilities of both panels, editors can efficiently fine-tune keyframe timing and values, ensuring precise control over the visual effects and animations in their projects.

View keyframes in the Effect Controls panel
Keyframes that you've added to a sequence clip can be seen in the Effect Controls panel. When an effect is collapsed, any effect that has keyframed attributes will show Summary Keyframe icons.

The effect heading is followed by summary keyframes that match each of the effect's specific property keyframes. Summary keyframes are there for reference only and cannot be altered.

- From a Timeline panel, pick a clip.
- To display the effects timeline, if needed, select the Show/Hide Timeline View button in the Effect Controls panel. Expand the Effect Controls panel if required in order to see the Show/Hide Timeline View button.
- To view the effect, you want to enlarge it by clicking the triangle to the left of its name in the Effect Controls panel. The timeline for Effect Controls shows the keyframes.
- (Details optional) Click the triangle that appears next to the Toggle Animation icon to display the Value and Velocity graphs for that effect property.

View keyframes and properties in a Timeline panel

If you've added keyframes to animate an effect, you can inspect them and their properties in a Timeline window. The keyframes unique to each clip can be seen in a Timeline window for both audio and video effects.

A Timeline panel can also show the keyframes for a whole track in the case of audio effects. Different properties can be displayed for every track or clip. But within a single clip or track, you can only see the keyframes for one attribute at a time.

A graph showing changes in keyframe values throughout the course of the clip or track is created by joining keyframe segments. Modifying segments and keyframes modifies the graph's form.

- (Optional) Click the triangle to the left of the track name to expand the track if it is compacted.
- Click the Show Keyframes button for a video track, then select any option from the menu:
  - Display Keyframes: shows the keyframes and graph for each video effect that has been applied to the track's clips. The clip name is accompanied with an effect menu where you can select which effect to display.
  - Display Opacity Handles: shows the keyframes and graph of the opacity effect for each of the track's clips.
  - Remove Keyframes: conceals the keyframes and graphs for each clip in the track.
- Click the Show Keyframes button for an audio track, then select any option from the menu:
  - Display Clip Keyframes: shows the keyframes and graph of any audio effects that have been applied to the track's clips. The clip name is accompanied with an effect menu where you can select which effect to display.
  - Show Clip Volume: Shows the volume effect's graph and keyframes for each clip in the track.
  - Show Track Keyframes: This shows the keyframes and graph for any audio effect that has been applied to the whole track. At the start of the music, an effect menu opens, allowing you to select which effect to view.
  - Show Track Volume shows the volume effect's keyframes and graph when it is applied to
  - Hide Keyframes: Hides the graphs and keyframes for all clips in the track.

- Optional: To have the effect menu show at the top of the track, enlarge the clip using the Zoom In option. To raise the track height, you can also drag the limits above and below the track name.

- Track header limits can be dragged to adjust a track's height (optional). Drag the track's top to make changes to a video track. Drag the track's bottom to move an audio file. Holding down the Shift key while dragging allows you to resize any expanded tracks.

- (Optional) Click the effect menu if in stages 2 and 3 you selected Show Keyframes, Show Clip Keyframes, or Show Track Keyframes. Next, choose the keyframe-containing effect.

- To examine the property of a keyframe in a tool tip, place the pointer exactly over it.

The location of the keyframe, together with its properties and settings from the Effect Controls panel, are shown in the tool tip. Utilize this data to precisely position keyframes. The value you've set for a keyframe is easily visible. Additionally, you may compare two or more keyframes' locations and values rapidly.

CHAPTER SIX
Audio Editing

Importing Audio

Digital audio clips that are saved as audio files or tracks in video files can be imported. Digital audio is recorded as binary data that computers may read on computer hard drives, audio CDs, or digital audio tape (DAT).

Use digital connections to transfer digital audio files to your computer in order to maintain the highest possible quality. Refrain from using your sound card to digitize the analog outputs from your audio sources.

Audio sample rates supported
Premiere Pro natively supports these audio sample rates:

- 8000 Hz
- 11025 Hz
- 22050 Hz
- 32000 Hz
- 44100 Hz
- 48000 Hz
- 96000 Hz

Every audio channel—including those contained in video clips—is processed by Premiere Pro as 32-bit floating-point data at the sequence sample rate. Maximum editing performance and audio quality are guaranteed by this processing.

Certain audio formats are conformed by Premiere Pro to the 32-bit format and sequence sample rate. If complying is necessary, it is completed the first time a file is imported into a project. It costs time and disk space to conform.

When conforming starts, a progress meter shows up at the lower right of the Premiere Pro window. Conformed audio is saved by Premiere Pro in CFA audio preview files.

By choosing a Scratch Disk location for Audio Previews in the Project Settings dialog box, you may choose where to save these audio preview files.

Before audio files are fully conformed, you can interact with them and even apply effects to them. Only the conforming portions of the files can be viewed, though.

Unconforming portions cannot be heard during playback.

The following guidelines dictate what kinds of audio are accepted:

Uncompressed audio

When uncompressed clips with natively supported sample rates are used in sequences with corresponding sample rates, Premiere Pro does not conform audio in those clips.

When used in sequences with different sample rates, Premiere Pro conforms audio in uncompressed clips. It is not until you export the sequences or make audio preview files that any conforming is completed.

Audio that was not captured in a natively supported sampling rate can be conformed in uncompressed formats using Premiere Pro.

In the majority of these situations, the audio will be up sampled to the closest supported sample rate or to a supported sample rate that is an even multiple of the sample rate of the original audio.

Since 11025Hz is the nearest supported rate and there isn't a supported rate that is an even multiple of 11024, it will, for instance, up sample a source at 11024Hz to 11025Hz.

Compression Audio

All compressed audio, including that contained in MP3, WMA, MPEG, and compressed MOV files, is compatible with Premiere Pro. This audio is conformed at the source file's sample rate. It will, for instance, conform an MP3 file at 44100Hz.

Nevertheless, the audio will play back at the sequence's sample rate without additional conforming if the conformed audio is used in a sequence with a non-matching sampling rate, such as when a 44100Hz clip is used in a 44000Hz sequence.

Provided that the file hasn't been relocated or renamed since it was conformed, Premiere Pro won't conform a file that was conformed in one sequence when you import it into another with the same audio sample rate.

The Media Cache Database contains the conform file locations for every file that Premiere Pro has conformed.

When a file with audio is initially imported into a project in Premiere Pro, it not only conforms certain files but also generates a PEK file for that file.

The audio waveforms in the Timeline panels are drawn using these PEK files. Premiere Pro uses the Media pane of the Preferences dialog box to save PEK files in the place designated for Media Cache Files.

Adjusting Volume Levels

Play the audio file as soon as you drop it into the Timeline. You could notice that the red lights in the Audio Meters go on.

These are alerts that your sound file is clipping and will be too loud. (Audio distortion results from clipping because the device's power rating is not met by the audio output power).

Thus, you must change the volume. You must follow the same steps for each of your audio clips if you have more than one.

- Double-clicking on the empty area to the left of the track or dragging the line at the bottom of the track down will both raise the track height.

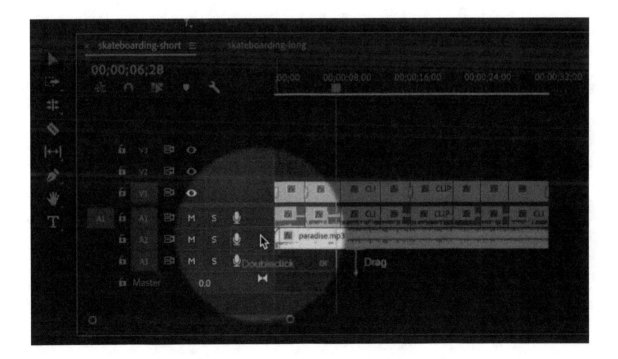

- Determine which line, yellow or white, crosses the clip.
- Drag it down to reduce the volume, and drag it up to boost it.

Advice: You might like the background temperature to be between -20 and -25.

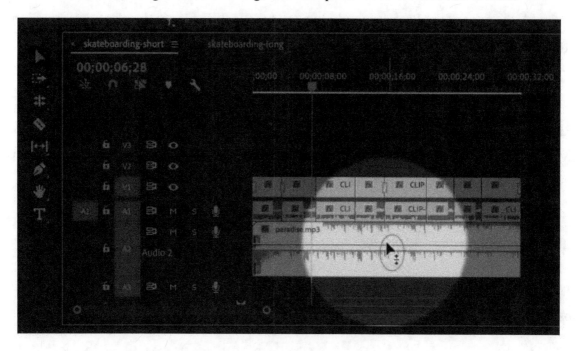

- If the audio on the other tracks is bothering you, mute it.

Adding Music and Sound Effects

Importing and Adding Music File
Import your music file after setting up your video's graphic elements.

- File > Import

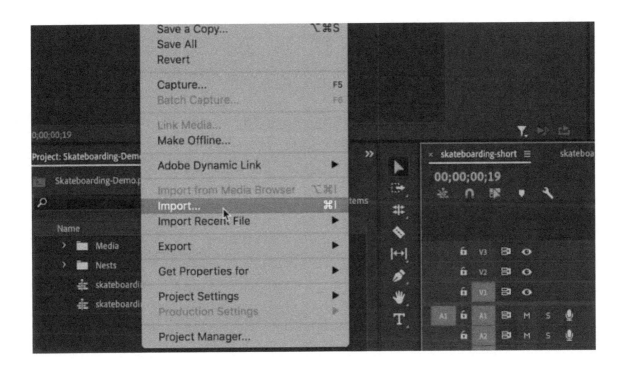

- Go to the file by navigating.

- Choose the File.

- Select Import.

- In the Project Panel, locate it.

- Place a music file into the Timeline that appears below the video clip.

CHAPTER SEVEN
Colour Correction and Grading

Correcting Exposure and Colour Balance

With the professional-grade colour correction tools available in Premiere Pro, you can edit video right on your timeline. The colour and brightness adjusting effects are located in the Video Effects bin's Colour Correction bin.

There are various applications for colour correcting adjustments:

- Edit video such that different shots seem to have been taken in the same locations.
- To make a clip look like it was shot at night rather than during the day, adjust the colours in it.
- A picture's exposure can be adjusted to bring back details from overexposed highlights.
- To add visual components to a clip, adjust the colour.
- Limit the colour spectrum of a clip to a specific range, like the broadcast-safe range.

The use of Colour Correction effects is identical to that of Standard effects. The Colour Correction effects are intended to make precise colour and luminance adjustments, even if other effects can also modify colour and brightness.

- The colour and brightness adjusting effects are located in the Video Effects bin's Colour Correction bin.
- The Effect Controls window is where you modify the properties of the effect.
- The colour effects, including Colour Correction, are clip-based. Nevertheless, you can use nesting sequences to apply them to several clips.
- Utilizing the Lumetri scopes to examine the brightness and chroma of a clip might be helpful for adjusting colour. To check your video levels as you make modifications, you can view a scope in a separate Lumetri panel.

Change Colour effect

The hue, brightness, and saturation of a variety of colours can be changed with the Change Colour effect.

These are the available choices for the Change Colour effect:

- **View:** The Change Colour effect's outcomes are displayed in View - Corrected Layer. The regions of the layer that will be altered are displayed by the Colour Correction Mask. The colour correction mask's white parts are altered the most, while its darkest areas are altered the least.

- **Hue Transform:** The hue adjustment in degrees.

- **Lightness Transform:** Positive values brighten the matched pixels, whereas negative values darken them in the lightness transform.

- **Saturation Transform:** Matching pixels with positive values are more saturated (going toward pure colour); matched pixels with negative values are less saturated (moving toward gray).

- **Colour To Change:** The colour that will be altered in the range's centre.

- **Matching Tolerance:** The amount of colour deviation from Colour To Match that results in a match.

- **Matching Softness:** The ratio of the effect's impact on mismatched pixels to how similar they are to Colour To Match.

- **Match Colours:** Establishes the colour space to be used for colour comparisons in order to assess similarity. RGB uses an RGB colour space to compare colours. Hue compares colour hues just, disregarding brightness and saturation; bright red and mild pink, for instance, match. Luminance (lightness) is ignored by chroma, which compares similarities between the two chrominance components.

- **Invert Colour Correction Mask**: To adjust which colours to affect, flip the mask used for colour correction.

Colour Balance Effect

Colour Balance adjusts the amount of red, green, and blue in an image's shadows, midtones, and highlights.

Maintain luminosity.

Maintains the average brightness of the image while altering the colour. This control maintains the image's tonal balance.

The Colour Balance (HLS) Effect

The Colour Balance (HLS) effect adjusts an image's hue, brightness, and saturation.

The Colour Balance (HLS) effect includes the following options:

- **Hue** - Determines the colour palette of the image.

- **Lightness** - Determines the brightness of the image.

- **Saturation** - Changes the image's colour saturation. The default value is zero, which has no effect on the colours. Negative numbers reduce saturation, while -100 converts the footage to grayscale. Values larger than zero result in more intense hues.

Applying Creative Looks

Premiere Pro's Lumetri Colour panel offers powerful tools for colour correction, but it also goes beyond that, allowing you to apply creative "Looks" to your videos. These Looks are presets that can dramatically alter the visual style of your footage, infusing it with a particular mood or theme.

Exploring Looks in the Lumetri Panel:
1. **Access the Lumetri Colour panel.** You'll typically find it in the Colour workspace or by clicking the "colour" button next to your program monitor.

2. **Navigate to the "Basic Correction" tab.** This tab often has a "Looks" section or dropdown menu.

3. **Browse the available Looks.** Premiere Pro offers a variety of built-in Looks, and you can also import custom Looks created by other users or downloaded from online sources.

Applying and Customizing Looks:
- Click on a Look thumbnail to preview its effect on your video in the program monitor.

- Once you find a Look you like, click on it again to apply it to your clip.

- The Look will be applied with default settings, but you can further customize it using the other controls within the Lumetri colour panel. These controls allow you to fine-tune the white balance, colour curves, saturation, and other aspects to achieve the desired visual style.

Benefits of Using Looks:
Save Time: Looks provide a quick and efficient way to establish a colour grade without having to make manual adjustments from scratch.

Consistency: Looks can help you maintain a consistent visual style across your entire project or a series of videos.

Creative Inspiration: Looks can spark creative ideas and offer starting points for developing your unique colour palette.

Finding and Importing Custom Looks:
- Several websites offer free and paid Looks compatible with Premiere Pro. Search online for "Premiere Pro Looks" or "LUTs" (Look Up Tables - a format commonly used for Looks).
- Once you've downloaded a Look file (usually in .cube or .3dlut format), import it into Premiere Pro by going to the "Browse" button next to the Looks dropdown menu and selecting the downloaded file.

Tips for Working with Looks:
- **Experiment!** Try different Looks to see how they transform your footage.
- **Don't be afraid to adjust.** Looks are a starting point, not a final destination. Use the Lumetri Colour panel controls to refine the Look and tailor it to your specific needs.
- **Consider your project's style.** Choose Looks that complement the overall tone and mood of your video.

By incorporating Creative Looks into your Premiere Pro workflow, you can efficiently enhance the visual style of your videos and achieve a cohesive aesthetic throughout your projects.

Using Adjustment Layers

Adjustment layers are an excellent technique to incorporate effects and colour grading into huge sections of your sequence. They can be accessed in your Project browser and added to the sequence in the same way that other clips and media are.

Because the adjustment layer is a standalone clip, it may be moved, chopped, turned off, or completely eliminated with a few clicks. If you've added an effect you don't like, just remove it from the adjustment layer.

Adjustment layers are extremely adaptable, giving editors more time to be creative. Using one can have an impact on other clips underneath or across an edit. Once you understand how to use them, you can easily try things out without having to undo everything afterward.

In Adobe® Premiere® Pro, you can utilize an adjustment layer to apply the same effect to several clips in the Timeline. When effects are applied to an adjustment layer, they affect all levels below it in the layer stacking order.

You can combine effects on a single adjustment layer. To control more effects, utilize numerous adjustment layers. Premiere Pro's adjustment layers work similarly to those in Adobe Photoshop and After Effects. Because adjustment layers can be utilized with so many different visual effects, it's hard to show you everything. In this step-by-step instruction, we'll use an adjustment layer to get an aged film effect throughout our sequence.

Step 1: Create a new adjustment layer.
Before you can add effects, you must first construct the adjustment layer. You can make as many as you need for your project.

- Navigate to File > New > Adjustment Layers. If it is greyed out, check that you have selected the Project browser and try again.
- You can also click the New Item button in the Project browser's bottom right corner and pick Adjustment Layer. The settings will automatically be the same as your sequence, so click OK.
- In the Project browser, right-click the new Adjustment Layer and choose Rename.
- Enter an appropriate name for your layer and press return.

Step 2: Include the Adjustment Layer in Your Sequence

As you can see, the adjustment layer is stored in your Project browser with your other clips and assets.

- In your Project browser, select the Adjustment Layer.

- Drag and drag it onto your timeline, ensuring sure it's stacked above the clip you want to apply effects to.

- Drag the ends of the Adjustment Layer out to cover the entire area where you wish to apply the changes.

Step 3: Add Your colour Grade.

It's a good idea to apply whatever colour grading you want before adding the effects, as this will set the tone for how the clip will seem.

- Go to the colour workspace.

- With your Adjustment Layer highlighted in the sequence, select the Lumetri colour panel on the right-hand side.

- Make your colour adjustments, remembering that the effect will be applied to every clip below it on the timeline.

Step 4: Add your effects.

The following step is to add your effects. In this example, we'll modify the colours, add noise, grain, and a vignette.

- On the right side of the Effects workspace, search for the effect you want.

- Drag and drop the effect to the Adjustment Layer.

- Change the effect parameters in the Effects Control Panel.

- Continue to add and tweak effects until you are satisfied with the appearance you have achieved.

CHAPTER EIGHT
Titles and Graphics

Creating Titles

To add titles, you must have a sequence open on the timeline in Premiere Pro. Move the playhead to the frame where you wish to place the title. Start by selecting the Text tool.

- Select the Typing tool.
- Type your words, and you'll notice a Title item emerge in the timeline above the clip.
- To open the Essential Graphics panel, right-click the title in the Program Monitor and select Edit Properties from the context menu. Here, you may edit your title's fonts, colours, and stylistic settings. Alternatively, double
- click the track item in the timeline.
- Use the Selection Tool to move or resize text and form layers in the Program Monitor.

Tips
You can adjust the duration of the Timeline's Title item by dragging it (the default is 5 seconds).

Choose shape tools to add graphical components.

Copy and paste your title into other places of the Timeline, then edit the text for each time.

Using Templates

Premiere Pro templates offer a fantastic way to expedite your video editing process and achieve professional-looking results, even for beginners. Here's a breakdown of what templates are and how to leverage them:

Templates are pre-designed projects containing various elements that you can easily customize to fit your video needs. it includes:

Motion graphics: Animated titles, intros, outros, transitions, and lower thirds (text overlays at the bottom of the screen).

A Motion Graphics template from your computer can be installed in the Essential Graphics panel's Local Templates folder. Unlike media, Motion Graphics templates do not reside in the Project panel.

- Drag and drag one or more templates into the Essential Graphics browser to install them in the Local Templates folder. Alternatively, you can install your MOGRTs by clicking the Install button in the lower right corner.
- Navigate to the folder where the Motion Graphics template is saved and click Open.

The template is copied to the Local Templates Folder and displayed in the Essential Graphics section.

Organize Motion Graphics templates

Create a library
Instead of saving your templates in the Local Templates folder, you can add them to libraries so they can be accessed from any device or shared with others.

To create a library, follow these steps:

- If the Libraries panel is not visible, go to Windows > Libraries to open it.
- Click the hamburger button next to Libraries and choose Create New Library from the drop-down menu.

- A textbox appears. Enter the new Library name, then select establish to establish a new Library.

Add a graphic to the library

You can add a Motion Graphics template to your library.

To add a MOGRT to your library, complete the steps below:

- Drag & drag libraries from the MOGRT view in the Essential Graphics panel to the locations view.
- You may alternatively right-click a MOGRT in the Essential Graphics panel and choose Copy to Library from the pop-up menu, then pick the library to which you want to add it.

Use Motion Graphics templates from Adobe Stock

Adobe Stock offers thousands of professionally created titles, lower thirds, transitions, and images for use in Premiere Pro. Browse Adobe Stock from the Essential Graphics tab to find and customize the exact graphic you need without leaving your current workstation.

Motion Graphics templates in Adobe Stock can be found in Premiere Pro's Essential Graphics or Libraries panels.

Search Adobe Stock for Motion Graphics templates using the Essential Graphics panel.
To search Adobe Stock for Motion Graphics templates, use the Essential Graphics panel:

1. In the Essential Graphics panel's Browse tab, pick Adobe Stock

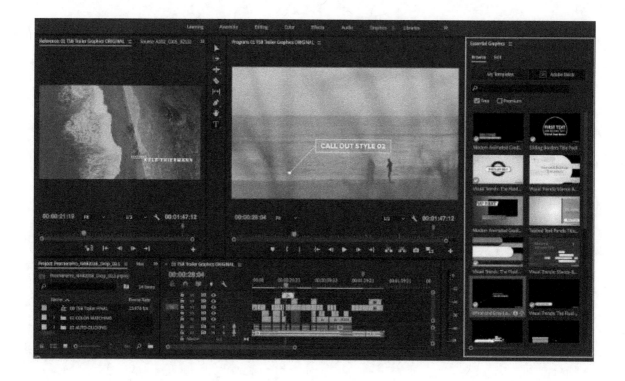

2. Enter your search term, then press Enter.

Premiere Pro presents Stocks findings in the form of pages. The number of pages is determined by the total number of results and how many things can fit on the browser panel at the selected thumbnail slider size. If you resize the thumbnail slider or the view, the number of pages changes to reflect the new size. To move through the Stock results, you can:

*   The previous and next arrows allow you to navigate to the next or previous page.
*   The text edit area can be used to navigate directly to a certain page.

3. To license the Motion Graphics template, drag it into your sequence or click the License and Download icon.

4. To learn more about a Motion Graphics template or get a preview of its animation, click the "i" icon beneath the thumbnail.

You can also license the Motion Graphics template to your Local Templates folder by clicking the License or Download icon in this window.

Working with the Essential Graphics Panel

Premiere Pro's Graphics workspace and Essential Graphics panel enable a sophisticated process for creating titles, graphics, and captions.

Open the Graphics workspace and the Essential Graphics panel.
To enter the Graphics workspace: Click Graphics in the workspace bar at the top of the screen, or choose Window > Workspaces > Graphics from the main menu.

To access the Essential Graphics panel: The Graphics workspace includes the Essential Graphics panel by default. If you don't see it, you can open it by selecting Window > Essential Graphics.

Parts of the Essential Graphics Panel

Use the tools in the Essential Graphics panel to work with text and shapes

Browse

This tab allows you to browse Motion Graphics templates (.mogrt files) in Adobe Stock. These are professionally created templates that can be quickly added to your timeline and customized. Adobe Stock is a marketplace for videos, motion graphics templates, pictures, and more.

Edit

You can use this tab to:

- Align and transform layers, modify appearance properties, adjust text properties, and more.
- Create keyframes for your Premiere Graphics (prgraphics).

- Modify accessible properties of your After Effects Graphics (aegraphics).

Create graphics.

Premiere Graphics, like Photoshop, supports many text, shape, and clip layers. Multiple layers can be stored within a single Graphic track item in your sequence. When you create a new layer, a graphic clip with that layer is added to the timeline, beginning at the playhead position. If you currently have a graphic track item selected, the following layer you build is added to the current graphic clip.

Any graphics you make in Premiere Pro can be saved as a Motion Graphics Template (.mogrt) in the Local Templates Folder, Local Drive, or Creative Cloud Libraries for sharing or reuse.

Create text layers   Create shape layers   Create clip layers

- Create a title with the Type tool in the Program Monitor or the New Layer > Text instructions in the Graphics Menu.
- Premiere Pro includes Pen, Rectangle, Ellipse, and Polygon Tools for generating freeform forms and paths.
- Include still photos and video clips as layers in your graphic.

Create a clip layer

You can include still images and video recordings as layers in your graphic. Clip layers can be created using the following methods:

- In the Essential Graphics panel's Edit tab, select the New Layer icon and then From File.
- In the application menu bar, go to Graphics > New Layer > From File.
- In your Project window, select either a static image or a video. Drag and drop that object into the Layers section of the Essential Graphics panel, or onto an existing Graphic in your Timeline.

CHAPTER NINE
Exporting your Project

Export Settings Overview

Focusing on content destinations allows you to swiftly and efficiently export completed films. You can use the optimum render settings for prominent social media networks like YouTube, TikTok, Facebook, and X. Alternatively, you can use the advanced settings to tailor your exports.

A. Choose export destinations B. Access output settings C. Customize export preset

1. Select the sequence you wish to export. When the Project panel is focused, Export mode utilizes the currently chosen sequence or clip as the source. Multiple selections are also supported, though with significant limits.

- Export preview is disabled.

- The export settings are applied to all sources

If other panels are focused, Export mode selects the Timeline panel's front-most open sequence as a source.

2. To open the Export workspace, select Export in Premiere Pro's header bar. To enter Export Mode, select File > Export > Media or press Cmd/Ctrl + M.

3. The export workflow progresses from left to right. Begin by selecting a video destination from the options in the left-hand column, such as TikTok, YouTube, Vimeo, or your local drive (Media File). Premiere Pro provides appropriate export options based on your destination.

4. Accept the default H.264 preset or select another preset from the Preset menu. You can also change the export settings and store your own custom presets. While individual options are available for all export parameters, Match Source defaults are frequently the best choice. These are adaptable presets that employ the same frame size, frame rate, and so on as your original sequence. Choose the High Bitrate preset to export a high-quality video.

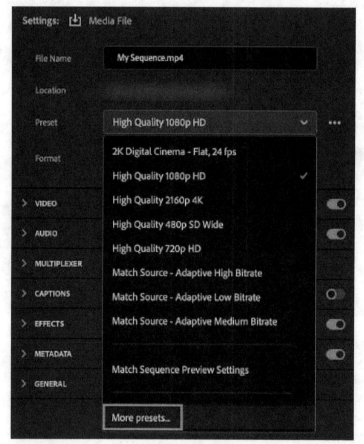

Choose export presets from the dropdown menu or click More presets to open the Preset Manager and manage your list of favourite presets

5. Use the Preview box to preview, scrub, and playback your media before exporting. You can also define a custom duration and manage how the source video fits into the output frame if you're exporting to a different size.

- Range allows you to set the duration of your exported video.

- Complete Source: the complete length of the sequence or clip will be exported.

- Source In/Out: If you have In/Out Points configured in your sequence or clip, those will be used for export.

- Work Area: Export the Work Area. Bar duration (sequences only).

- Custom: respects custom In/Out Points set in export mode.

- Scaling allows you to change how the source fits into the produced frame when exporting to a different frame size. Scaling allows you to change how the source fits into the produced frame when exporting to a different frame size.

- Scale to fit resizes the source to fit the output frame without distorting or cropping pixels. Black bars may be noticed.

- Scale to fill: resizes the source to completely fill the output frame, leaving no black bars. Some pixels may be clipped.

- Stretch to fill: stretches the source to fill the entire output frame, leaving no black bars or chopped pixels. The frame aspect is not maintained; therefore, the movie may appear distorted.

6. Click Report

Exporting for Different Platforms

Once you've meticulously edited your video in Premiere Pro, it's time to export it for the world to see! But here's the catch: different platforms have varying requirements for video formats, resolutions, and bitrates. Fear not, for Premiere Pro offers robust export options to ensure your video looks stunning on any platform.

Understanding Export Settings:
- **Format:** This refers to the container that holds your video and audio data. Common export formats include MP4 (H.264), MOV, and AVI.

- **Resolution:** This determines the number of pixels displayed horizontally and vertically, impacting video quality and file size. Common resolutions include 1080p (1920x1080 pixels) and 4K (3840x2160 pixels).

- **Frame Rate:** The number of images (frames) displayed per second. Standard frame rates are 23.98 fps (frames per second) for film-like projects and 29.97 fps for video content.

- **Bitrate:** This controls the amount of data used to encode each second of video, affecting both quality and file size. Higher bitrates result in better quality but larger files.

Exporting for Specific Platforms:

- **YouTube:** Use the H.264 format, with resolutions like 1080p or 720p depending on your video's needs. Choose a bitrate appropriate for the chosen resolution (consult YouTube's recommendations).

- **Vimeo:** Similar to YouTube, Vimeo accepts H.264 format videos. You can choose from various resolutions and bitrate options based on your video's specifications.

- **Social Media:** Each platform has its own recommendations. Generally, H.264 format and lower resolutions (720p or lower) with moderate bitrates are suitable for social media uploads due to file size limitations.

- **Blu-ray Discs:** For high-quality archival or physical media distribution, export using formats compatible with Blu-ray standards, typically MPEG-2 with specific resolution and bitrate requirements.

Premiere Pro's Export Options:

- **File > Export > Media:** This is the standard path for exporting your video project in Premiere Pro.

- **Export Settings:** This window allows you to configure various settings like format, resolution, frame rate, bitrate, and more.

- **Presets:** Premiere Pro offers built-in presets optimized for common export scenarios like YouTube, Vimeo, and social media platforms. These presets are a great starting point, but you can customize them further if needed.

Tips for Successful Exports:

- **Match platform requirements:** Always research the specific format, resolution, and bitrate recommendations for your target platform.

- **Balance quality and file size:** Aim for a good compromise between video quality and file size, considering upload limitations or storage constraints.

- **Use high-quality source footage:** The quality of your exported video ultimately depends on the quality of your source clips.

- **Test your exports:** Before uploading to your chosen platform, play back your exported video to ensure everything looks and sounds as intended.

By understanding these export settings and effectively utilizing Premiere Pro's features, you can tailor your video exports for any platform, ensuring your creation reaches its audience in the best possible quality.

Sharing Your Work

There are four possible ways to transfer files from Adobe Premiere Pro:

1. Adobe Creative Cloud
2. Email (Premiere Pro Project Manager),
3. Shared network drives,
4. MASV Panel

1. Adobe Creative Cloud

If you own Premiere Pro, you also have access to 100 GB of storage in Adobe Creative Cloud. Let us take advantage of this.

- Open the Creative Cloud application.
- Navigate to the Files tab at the top of the window.
- Click the Open sync folder button at the bottom left of the window. This folder is located on your PC and connects to your cloud storage.

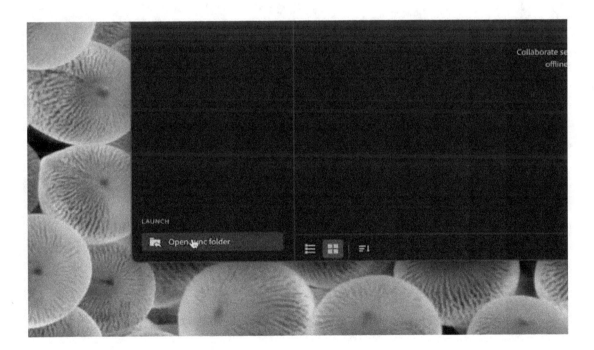

- Drag and drag the files and folders you wish to share. They will sync, and you will be able to access them from any computer you log onto.

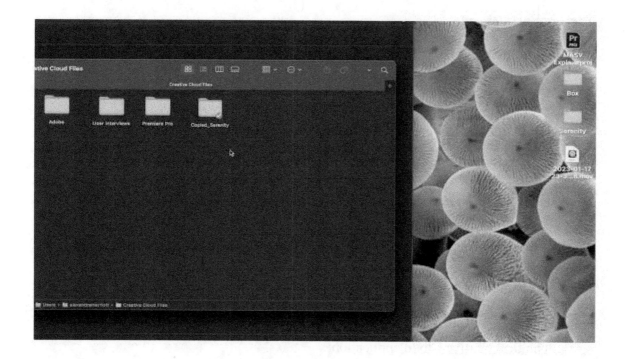

- Go to the Creative Cloud on your browser. Send your file(s) with a direct invite or a link.

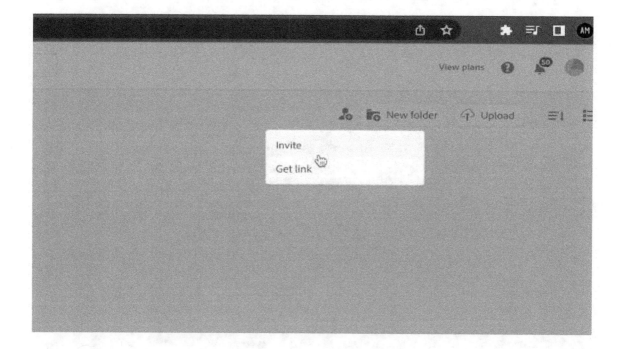

You may also set up automatic backups of your project data to the cloud. This is great for working on different machines with your most recent cut.

- Open Premiere Pro.
- Go to the Premiere Pro menu at the top of the screen.

- Then, navigate to Settings > Auto Save.
- In the Preferences box, make sure the Save Backup Project to Creative Cloud option is checked.

2. Email (Premiere Pro Project Manager)

You may just attach the Premiere Pro project file to an email and send it along. It is usually tiny enough to attach directly to an email. This works best when the recipient already has a copy of the source files and wants to relink them. This will not always be the case.

If they do not have the essential files, you must first collect and save the Premiere project, which includes all files used in the sequence. To accomplish this, take these steps:

- Open Premiere Pro.
- Navigate to File > Project Manager.

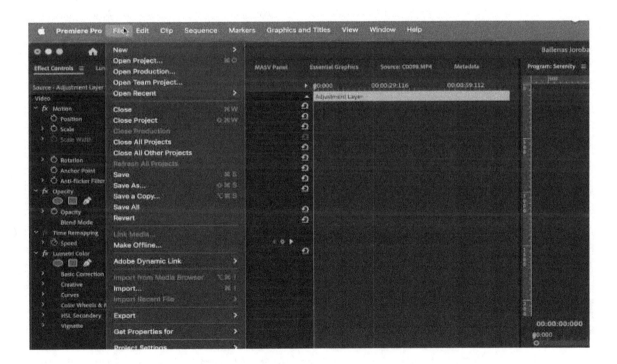

- In the new window at the top, select the sequence you wish to share.
- Under Resulting Project, select Collect Files and Copy to a New Location. This will do precisely what it says: we will have a copy of all used files in the same location as our project.
- To avoid unnecessary files taking up space, make sure Exclude Unused Clips is set on the right side of the Options window.

- Under Destination Path, select your folder's destination.

- (Optional) Calculate how much Disk Space the finished folder will take up.

- When Premiere Pro prompts you to save the project, click OK, followed by Yes.

You now have the project file and all of the necessary files to open it. So, how do you transmit it by email?

Depending on the size of your finished folder, you may be able to compress and send it immediately. However, you will most likely need a large file-transferring solution, such as Google Drive, WeTransfer, or MASV, to deliver the large folder of collected files to the recipient's email.

3. Shared Network drive

A shared network drive is primarily utilized in office settings since it allows several machines to access it from a single location. Share network drives typically feature a large amount of storage space, allowing you to quickly share data with your business colleagues.

Follow these extremely basic steps:

- Drag and drop the project or gathered files folder onto the shared network drive folder.

- Let your teammates know when it's ready so they may download a copy.

4. MASV Panel

It's quite simple to use MASV to send your full Premiere Pro project with files, and you may do so right within Premiere. Plus, it's the quickest way to transfer files, allowing you to be more productive.

1. Download the MASV Panel plugin from Adobe Exchange.

2. Once downloaded, launch Premiere Pro.
3. Navigate to Windows > Extensions > MASV Panel.
4. Login to your account.
5. Send the project:

If you only want to send one item from your bin or a rendered sequence, select Add Item in the popup box.

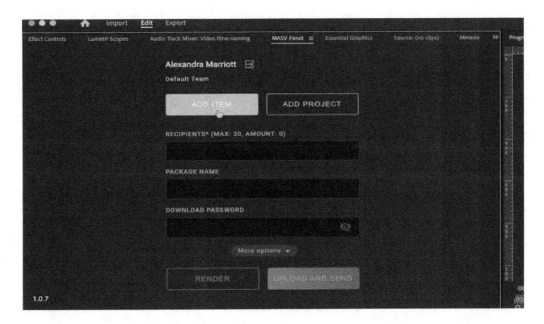

88

To save your Premiere project with all files, select Add Project. It automatically organizes all of the files and metadata into a single folder for convenient media linking.

1. Enter the email addresses for the recipients.
2. Provide a name for your bundle.
3. If you want to safeguard your content, set a password.

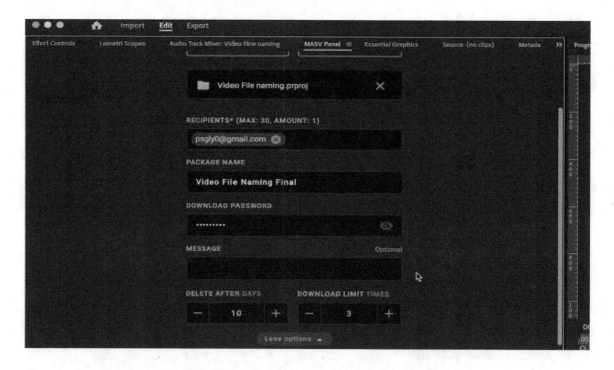

1. If you want to provide further information, click More options.
2. Click Upload and Send!

CHAPTER TEN
Advanced Techniques

Multi-camera Editing

Multicam editing is the technique of editing video of a single scene or subject shot from multiple cameras and perspectives. Showing the same event or subject from several perspectives makes the video more lively and visually appealing to your audience.

Using this technique also allows you to exhibit the same scene from multiple views. Multiple cameras are frequently utilized in music videos, soap operas, reality television, live performance records, corporate videos, and weddings.

Multi-camera editing workflow

1. Create a project.
On the Premiere Pro Welcome screen, click New Project or File > New Project. In the New Project dialog box, name the project and click OK to accept the defaults.

2. Import footage.
Select File > Import. In the Import dialog box that displays, select the directory holding your video and audio files. Choose the files to import and click Open.

3. Develop a multi-camera source sequence.
You can make a multicam source sequence in the following ways:

- Select a bin containing assets and a sync technique from the Create Multi-camera Source Sequence dialog box. All clips in the bin are processed using the sync approach and sorted alpha-numerically in the final source sequence.

- Select assets manually and select a sync mechanism from the Create Multi-camera Source Sequence dialog box. The order in which you chose the clips determines the order of the eventual source sequence.

To use the Create Multi-camera Source Sequence dialog box, choose your clips or bin from the Project panel. Then, right-click (Windows) or Ctrl-click (Mac OS) on the selected clips and select Create Multi-camera Source Sequence from the context menu.

4. Establish a multi-camera target sequence.
Create an editing sequence with the audio mix track that is appropriate for the desired output format (stereo or multichannel). Make sure to select the correct Mix Track type at the start, as

you cannot change it later in the Sequence Settings menu. For timeline audio tracks, employ stereo tracks for all-stereo workflows and mono tracks for multichannel workflows. Make sure you examine the audio mixing method before dropping the multi-camera clips onto the existing Timeline.

Tip: If the timeline is currently empty, put a multi-camera clip into it to update the sequence parameters to match the multi-camera clip settings. This step saves the previously specified Audio Tracks and Mix Tracks.

It is not suggested that you use the Sequence from Clip command or drag a multi-camera clip to the new sequence button in the Project panel. It generates a sequence of adaptive audio tracks, which are commonly utilized in complex audio routing operations.

5. Turn on multi-camera editing in the Program Monitor.
To enable multi-camera target sequence for multi-camera editing, click the icon and select Multi-camera from the Program Monitor's pop-up menu. The Program Monitor is now in multi-camera mode. In multi-camera mode, you may examine footage from all cameras at the same time and switch between them to select material for the final sequence.

6. Allow recording of multi-camera edits.
Turn the Multi-camera Record toggle switch on. If the button is not displayed in the button bar, launch the Button Editor by clicking "+" in the Program Monitor's lower-right corner. Drag the Multi-camera Record button onto the button bar.

7. Edit the multiple-camera scene.
To begin playback in the Program Monitor or Timeline panel, press the spacebar or select the Play-Stop toggle button. While the sequence is playing, press the number key on the main keyboard to switch to the camera at that number.

8. Adjust and refine modifications.
After recording your multi-camera edit, you can do the following:

- Rerecord the closing scene, replacing clips with footage from one of the other cameras.
- Edit the multi-camera source sequence in the same way you would any other sequence, using conventional editing tools and techniques, adding effects, and compositing with multiple tracks and adjustment layers.
- Change the cameras once they have already been recorded.
- Cut to a different perspective.

Export the multiple-camera sequence.
With the sequence active in the Program Monitor or Timeline window, go to File > Export > Media. Enter your export parameters and click Export, or click Queue to send the sequence to Adobe Media Encoder for encoding.

Use the Multi-Camera Source Sequence dialogue box.
To merge clips with shared In/Out points or overlapping timecode, use the Create Multi-camera Source Sequence dialog box. You can also combine clips with audio waveforms and markers.

Multi-Camera Source Sequence Name
You can name your multi-camera source sequence after the main video or audio clip in the sequence. From the pop-up menu, select the appropriate option to add "Multicam" or a custom name to the primary video or audio name. Alternatively, pick Custom from the pop-up menu and type a custom name into the text field.

Multi-Camera follows Nest Setting.
You can use the sequence contextual menu option named Multi-Camera Follows Nest Setting to determine if the option to cut in sequences as nests or individual clips should be applied to multi-Camera sources when they are cut into a sequence, or disregarded.

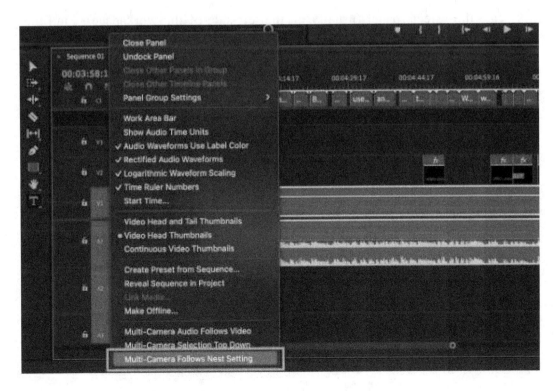

Time Remapping

While Dynamic Link excels at connecting Premiere Pro with After Effects for complex animation, Premiere Pro itself boasts a powerful tool called Time Remapping for manipulating the speed of your video clips. This section delves deeper into time remapping and its creative applications:

The Essence of Time Remapping:
Time remapping allows you to alter the playback speed of any clip within your Premiere Pro timeline. You can achieve effects like:

- Slow motion: Emphasize specific moments, heighten tension, or reveal details otherwise missed at regular speed.
- Fast motion: Condense lengthy sequences, add dynamism, or create a comedic effect.
- Custom speed variations: Gradually ramp up the speed for an energetic buildup or slow down subtly for a more contemplative mood.

Accessing Time Remapping:

There are two ways to access time remapping for a clip in Premiere Pro:

1. Right-click on the clip in your timeline and select Show Clip Keyframes > Time Remapping > Speed.
2. Locate the Effects panel (usually on the left side of the workspace). Find the Time Remapping effect and drag and drop it onto your clip in the timeline.

The Rubber Band Metaphor:

Premiere Pro visualizes clip speed with a horizontal line in the timeline, often referred to as the "rubber band." The centre of the rubber band represents the clip's original speed (100%).

- Dragging the rubber band upwards increases the playback speed (fast motion).
- Dragging the rubber band downwards decreases the playback speed (slow motion).

Creating Speed Variations (Keyframes):

While you can simply adjust the overall speed of a clip by dragging the rubber band, time remapping's true power lies in creating variations. Here's how:

- Position the play head at the point in your clip where you want the speed to change.
- Click on the diamond-shaped icon above the rubber band to create a speed keyframe. This essentially marks a specific point on the timeline where the playback speed will adjust.
- Repeat step 2 to create additional keyframes at different points in your clip.
- Drag the rubber band up or down at each keyframe to set the desired speed for that specific section.

Using the Selection Tool:

- After creating keyframes, switch to the **Selection tool** (arrow icon).
- Clicking and dragging between existing keyframes allows you to fine-tune the speed curve between those points, creating smooth transitions between different speeds.

Reversing Clips:

An interesting application of time remapping is reversing clips. Hold **Ctrl/Cmd** (depending on your operating system) while dragging a **speed keyframe to the left** beyond the clip's start point. This will reverse the clip's playback direction within that section.

By mastering time remapping in Premiere Pro, you gain a powerful tool to manipulate the pacing of your videos, adding dynamism, emphasizing key moments, and creating a more engaging viewing experience.

Using Dynamic Link with Adobe After Effects

Previously, exchanging media assets between post-production programs required you to render and export your work in one application before importing it into another. The workflow was inefficient and time-consuming.

If you wanted to edit the original asset, you simply rendered and exported it again. Multiple rendered and exported versions of an asset eat disk space and can cause file management issues.

Dynamic Link provides an alternative to this workflow. You may make dynamic linkages between After Effects and Adobe Premiere Pro.

Creating a dynamic link is much like importing any other sort of asset. To assist you recognize dynamically linked objects, they display unique icons and label colours. These programs create projects that save dynamic links.

Create and link to After Effects compositions with Dynamic Link
You can create new After Effects compositions, and dynamically link to them from Adobe Premiere Pro. You can also dynamically link to existing After Effects compositions from Adobe Premiere Pro.

Create a composition from clips in Adobe Premiere Pro
Adobe Premiere Pro allows you to replace selected clips with a dynamically connected After Effects composition based on those clips. The new composition inherits Adobe Premiere Pro's sequence settings.

- Open Premiere Pro and choose the clips you wish to replace.
- Right-click on any of the selected clips.
- Select Replace with After Effects Composition.

After Effects is launched (if it is not already open), and a new connected composition is generated.

Create a dynamically linked composition from Adobe Premiere Pro
When you create a new dynamically linked composition in Adobe Premiere Pro, it starts After Effects. After Effects then generates a project and composition with the same size, pixel aspect ratio, frame rate, and audio sample rate as the original project.

(If After Effects is already open, it will build a composition in the current project.) The new composition name is derived from the Adobe Premiere Pro project name, followed by Linked Comp:

- In Adobe Premiere Pro, select File > Adobe Dynamic Link > New After Effects Composition. Premiere Pro 2014 allows you to import compositions via Media Browser. For more information, go to the Premiere Pro sections listed below:
  - Import files with Media Browser
  - Adobe Dynamic Link

- If the After Effects Save As dialog box displays, enter the name and location of the After Effects project, then click Save.

CHAPTER ELEVEN
Troubleshooting and Resources
Common Issues and Solutions

Common issues you might encounter in Premiere Pro and their solutions include:

Choppy playback: This can be frustrating when trying to edit smoothly. Here are some solutions:

- Reduce the preview resolution: Premiere Pro allows you to preview your video at different resolutions. Lowering the resolution reduces the processing power required for playback, making it smoother.
- Disable preview effects: Previewing with effects like colour correction or motion graphics can also slow things down. Try disabling them while editing to improve playback performance.
- Upgrade your hardware: If you're constantly experiencing choppy playback, even with lower resolutions and effects disabled, it might be a sign your computer doesn't meet the recommended specs for Premiere Pro. Consider upgrading your hardware, particularly your graphics card and RAM.

Missing media files: If you see error messages about missing media files, it means Premiere Pro can't locate the video clips or audio files you used in your project. This can happen if you've moved or renamed the files. Here's how to fix it:

- Relink the media files: Premiere Pro allows you to relink missing files. Use the "Browse" button next to the error message to locate the files in their new location.

Audio glitches: Audio problems can be distracting in your videos. Here's how to troubleshoot them:

- Check audio sample rate and format compatibility: Make sure your audio files have compatible sample rates and formats with your project settings. Premiere Pro might not play incompatible audio correctly.

Project crashes: Premiere Pro crashes can be a real headache, especially if you haven't saved your work recently. Here are some potential causes and solutions:

- **Low memory:** Premiere Pro requires a significant amount of RAM to run smoothly. Close any unnecessary programs running in the background to free up memory.

- **Corrupted project files:** In rare cases, project files themselves can become corrupted. Try creating a new project and importing your edits or media from the problematic project.
- **Software conflicts:** Outdated graphics card drivers or conflicting software can sometimes cause crashes. Update your graphics drivers and check for any known compatibility issues.

Warp stabilizer issues: Warp stabilizer is a great tool for smoothing out shaky footage, but it can sometimes have problems:

- **Speed limitation:** Warp stabilizer cannot be applied to clips that have already been speed-adjusted. To use warp stabilizer, you'll need to nest the clip (create a sub-clip) and apply the stabilizer before adjusting the speed.
- **Artifacts:** In some cases, warp stabilizer might introduce unwanted artifacts or distortions in your video. Experiment with the warp stabilizer settings to find a balance between smoothness and image quality.

Export problems: When exporting your final video, you might encounter issues:

- **Incompatible codecs:** If you're planning to share your video online or use it for a specific platform, make sure you choose an export format and codec compatible with those requirements. Premiere Pro offers various export presets for common uses like YouTube or social media.
- **Incorrect export settings:** Double-check your export settings, such as frame size, frame rate, and bitrate, to ensure they match your project settings and desired output quality.

Audio and video out of sync: This can be a real immersion breaker for viewers. Here are some possible causes:

- **Variable frame rate (VFR) footage:** Some cameras record video with variable frame rates, which can cause syncing issues in Premiere Pro. There are tools within Premiere Pro to interpret and correct VFR footage.
- **Incorrect editing:** Make sure you haven't accidentally added gaps or overlaps in your editing that throw off the audio and video sync.

By being aware of these common issues and their solutions, you can troubleshoot problems efficiently and keep your Premiere Pro workflow running smoothly.

Useful Online Resources

Here are some useful online resources to help you with Premiere Pro:

Official Adobe Resources:
- **Adobe Premiere Pro Help Centre:** A comprehensive resource with in-depth articles, tutorials, and troubleshooting guides directly from Adobe.

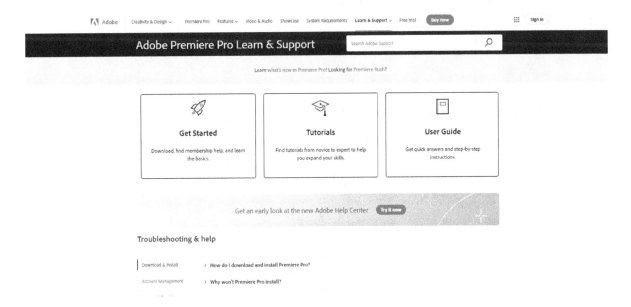

- **Adobe Premiere Pro Tutorials:** Official video tutorials created by Adobe, covering various aspects of Premiere Pro from beginner to advanced topics.

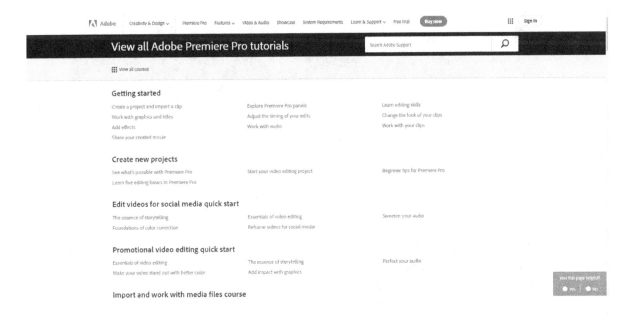

Video Tutorial Channels:

- **Adobe Premiere Pro YouTube Channel:** Offers a wide range of video tutorials on Premiere Pro features, tips, and tricks.

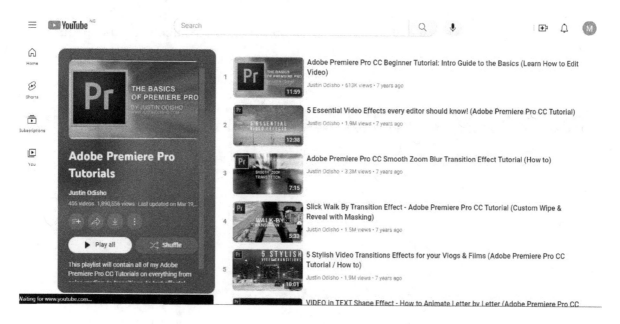

- **Learn Premiere Pro:** A popular YouTube channel by Iain Lain with high-quality tutorials for all skill levels.

- **Cinecom.net:** Another excellent YouTube channel by Chris Plush with in-depth tutorials and workflow guides for Premiere Pro.

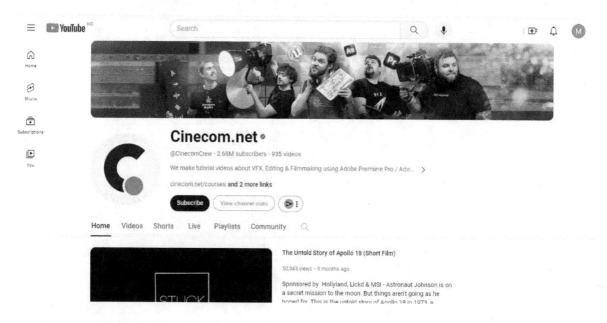

Online Communities and Forums:

- **r/premiere subreddit:** A subreddit dedicated to Premiere Pro with discussions, troubleshooting advice, and user-created content.

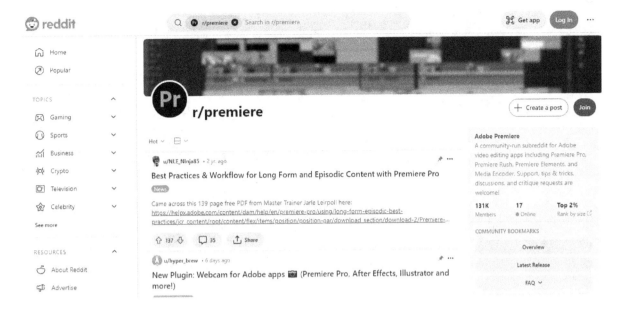

- **Adobe Premiere Pro User Forums:** The official Adobe forum for Premiere Pro, where you can ask questions, get help from other users and Adobe staff, and stay updated on the latest news.

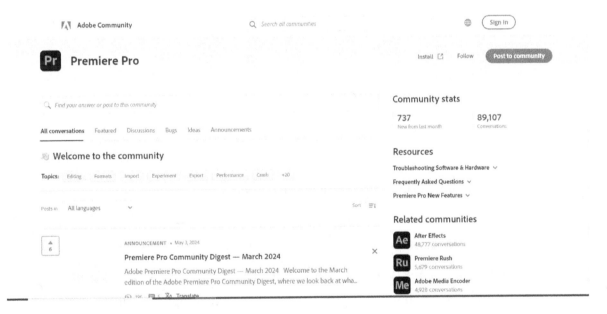

Additional Resources:

- **Noble Desktop:** Offers free resources like blog articles and YouTube tutorials on Premiere Pro, with some paid courses available as well.

NewBlue FX: An article compiling useful resources for Premiere Pro, including free tutorials and forums.

Remember, this is not an exhaustive list, and there are many other fantastic resources available online. The best resources for you will depend on your learning style and specific needs.

Community Forums and Support

Here are some helpful online communities and forums specifically focused on Premiere Pro support:

- **Adobe Premiere Pro User Forums:** This is the official Adobe forum for Premiere Pro. It's a great place to get help from other users and Adobe staff, ask questions, and stay updated on the latest news and developments related to Premiere Pro.
- **r/premiere subreddit:** This subreddit is a thriving online community dedicated to Premiere Pro. You'll find discussions on a wide range of topics, troubleshooting advice from experienced users, and user-created content like Premiere Pro tips and tricks.
- **Creative COW - Premiere Pro forum:** Creative COW is a well-established online community for creative professionals, and their Premiere Pro forum is a valuable resource. You can find discussions on various aspects of Premiere Pro, connect with other video editors, and learn from their experiences.

These are just a few of the many online communities that can provide support and resources for Premiere Pro users. Here are some additional tips for getting the most out of these forums:

- **Search before you post:** Chances are, your question has already been asked and answered in the forum. Take some time to search the forum archives before creating a new post.

- **Be clear and concise in your question:** The more specific you are about your issue, the easier it will be for others to help you.

- **Provide context:** When asking for help, include details about your project, the specific problem you're encountering, and any troubleshooting steps you've already tried.

- **Be polite and respectful:** Remember, everyone in the forum is there to learn and help each other.

By following these tips, you can effectively leverage online communities to get the support you need and enhance your Premiere Pro skills.

CONCLUSION

Adobe Premiere Pro is at the forefront of professional video editing software, functioning as a vital tool in a variety of industries.

Adobe Premiere Pro emerges as the foundation of professional video editing, renowned for its industry-standard status in film, television, the online, and social media. Its user-friendly timeline-based interface allows for smooth arrangement and manipulation of video clips, which is supplemented with a plethora of functions such as editing, color correction, effects, and audio mixing. Premiere Pro, as part of the Adobe Creative Cloud package, connects smoothly with other Adobe apps, demonstrating its versatility and accessibility through variable subscription arrangements.

Premiere Pro has a diversified user base that includes video editing companies, broadcast media organizations, marketing and advertising professionals, filmmakers, educators, students, and aspiring content creators. Its universal appeal cuts across professional boundaries, appealing to both seasoned professionals and ardent novices alike.

Premiere Pro plays a critical role in the world of video editing, allowing users to create fascinating tales, increase viewer engagement, rigorously control pacing, and tailor content to different audiences. Its broad set of tools and features is the foundation for creating seamless, polished video projects across a wide range of genres and platforms.

In addition to its basic features, Premiere Pro includes a plethora of supplemental materials meant to enhance the user experience and aid skill development. Premiere Pro supports a dynamic learning environment favorable to continuous growth and expertise, offering full support for a wide range of file types, troubleshooting solutions, and a plethora of online learning resources.

Mastering Premiere Pro requires patience, dedication, and discovery. While the software's richness and complexity may create a learning curve, users are urged to view experimenting and creativity as essential components of the learning process. Effective structure, thorough consideration of the intended audience, and a sense of fun are essential for realizing Premiere Pro's full potential.

www.ingramcontent.com/pod-product-compliance
Lightning Source LLC
LaVergne TN
LVHW081759050326
832903LV00027B/2025

* 9 7 9 8 3 2 5 6 4 2 8 0 7 *